BIO JAMES

#23

Emmett James

a memoir

Admit One

My Life in Film

To protect certain people, some names of individuals and locations in this book have been altered, and some characters are composites.

Published by Fizzypop Productions, LLC
Los Angeles, CA
www.fizzypopproductions.com

Distributed by Emerald Book Company

For ordering information or special discounts for bulk purchases, please contact Emerald Book Company at PO Box 91869, Austin, TX 78709, 512.891.6100.

Edited by Daria James
Design and composition by Fizzypop Productions, LLC
Cover design by Fizzypop Productions, LLC

Publisher's Cataloging-In-Publication Data
(Prepared by The Donohue Group, Inc.)

James, Emmett.

  Admit one : my life in film : a memoir / Emmett James. — 2nd ed.
    p. 216; cm.

  Previous ed. published: Tucson, Ariz. : Wheatmark Books, 2007.
  ISBN: 978-0-9842581-0-9

1. James, Emmett. 2. Actors—Great Britain—Biography. 3. Motion picture industry. I. Title.

PN2598.J29 A3 2010
792.028/092   2009938274

Part of the Tree Neutral™ program, which offsets the number of trees consumed in the production and printing of this book by taking proactive steps, such as planting trees in direct proportion to the number of trees used: www.treeneutral.com

First Edition published 2007
Wheatmark Books, Tucson, Arizona

Printed in the United States of America on acid-free paper

10 11 12 13 14   10 9 8 7 6 5 4 3 2 1

Second Edition

For D.
She took some jumbled words and a jumbled life,
and made them all make sense.

*"Life is not what one lived, but what
one remembers and how one remembers it
in order to recount it."*

Gabriel García Márquez

"Enter the dream-house, brothers and sisters,
leaving your debts asleep, your history at the door:
This is the home for heroes, and this loving
darkness a fur you can afford."

Cecil Day-Lewis

Cecil Day-Lewis spoke of the arrival of the greatest form of entertainment known to the nineteenth century: moving pictures. In 1968, Day-Lewis was appointed Poet Laureate of Great Britain, a position he held until his death four years later. Unfortunately, he would die before his son, Academy Award winner Daniel Day-Lewis, would become one of the finest film actors to embrace the next century, one of the most sought after thespians of the so-called dream-house.

This is a book of my memories, and though I did encounter points of contention (mainly where my memory placed events out of sequence), recollection has its own valid tale to tell. Nevertheless, while committing my memory to paper, I have done my utmost to present an honest account of the events as I recall them.

❧

CONTENTS

ॐ

INTRODUCTION

If I could tell you just one thing about my life it would be this: My alter ego was once a very famous man.

While reflecting fondly on the films that are most memorable to me, I am struck by one pertinent truth (thanks to the 20/20 hindsight of adulthood). That fact is this: A film itself, though unalterable once the physical reel is printed and unleashed, changes continually in the reel of our memory.

One of the earliest critics of drama, the ancient philosopher Aristotle, postulates in *Poetics* that there are really only six basic points to every story; everything else is merely a variation on a theme. Whether you agree or disagree with his theory, picking up any present-day film guide serves at least to prove that we have accumulated a voluminous set of variations to date. (If only Aristotle had been able to witness Bruce Willis make a career out of mastering hundreds of variants using just one basic story... or maybe it's better that he was spared.)

I wrote this book under the guise that the key to experiencing film, without losing relevance and meaning, is context. The environment, mood, personal history and circumstances in which a person sees a film changes that film in a necessary, unique, and exciting way. It creates a whole new story—a living, breathing film. The film of one's life. That being said, I present to you my story. I hope you will in turn recount your own with similar reverence.

PROLOGUE:
THE BEST OF THE BEST,
AND AN OPEN LETTER
TO STEVEN SEAGAL

Here is a list of my *best of the best*; the ten most enduring films that I experienced as a kid:

1. *The Wizard of Oz*

2. *The (Original) Star Wars Trilogy*

3. *E.T.*

4. *Rocky III*

5. *Raiders of the Lost Ark*

6. *The Jungle Book*

7. *Grease*

8. *The Karate Kid*

9. *Ghostbusters*

10. *The Golden Voyage of Sinbad*

It goes without saying that you won't see any of your films on that list, Mr. Steven Seagal; these were the movies that had a real emotional impact on me. I imagine that you, Mr. Seagal, would creep onto my list of worst horror movies ever, at a real stretch, but that's about it. The aforementioned, coveted spots are set aside for films creating an experience of sheer joy, wonderment, and exhilaration for the lucky audience, unlike anything Steven Seagal has EVER been a part of.

The days of seeing pure nonsense movies are gone for me—no more will I sit through BMX Bandits, Howard the Duck, Mannequin 2, Teen Wolf, Beat Street, or any movie where a monkey is the star. I know now with perfect hindsight and basic arithmetic that a real monkey in a leading role equals a bad movie. You shouldn't even bother wasting your time if one such movie crosses your path. Under Siege (parts I and II), or any of Jean-Claude Van Damme's movies, fall into the same category, all with similar primate lead actors. Farewell to each and every one of you.

Feeling cinematic happiness really meant something to me back in my childhood. I will assume it meant something to each of us. Steven Seagal's films don't give anyone that; watching them is just disheartening and quite unnecessary, like pissing down your own leg. The only thing of his that ever made me happy, or that I ever wanted to watch, was…

Kelly LeBrock.

Great movies are films like: **It Happened One Night, Stagecoach, Some Like It Hot, Citizen Kane, Singin' in the Rain, The Godfather, Sullivan's Travels, Annie Hall, Red River, Guess Who's Coming to Dinner, The Best Years of Our Lives, Taxi Driver, The Sting, Paths of Glory, Vertigo, The Hustler, Sunset Boulevard, Bonnie and Clyde, The Wild Bunch, Kramer vs. Kramer, Born Yesterday, Gone with the Wind, The Graduate, A Place in the Sun, A Streetcar**

Named Desire, To Kill a Mockingbird, One Flew Over the Cuckoo's Nest, Goodfellas, A Patch of Blue, 12 Angry Men, King Kong, City Lights, Blade Runner, Reservoir Dogs, and *Midnight Cowboy.* The mere mention of these film titles sets off a chain reaction of thoughts, quickly progressing to feelings in everyone and anyone lucky enough to have experienced them.

Celluloid is about dreams, movies are about fantasy, and motion pictures are about things you couldn't possibly even imagine in your wildest dreams, brought vividly to life in front of your very eyes. Cinema is about capturing the good and bad things that are pivotal in people's lives. There is, though, an unwritten rule in Hollywood that you obviously haven't been told about, Mr. Seagal...movies should never be as mind-numbingly dull as the day-to-day of real life. We can watch that sad reel anytime we want.

Mr. Seagal, I'm having a party, and you're just not invited... Sorry about that, Stevie.

coming attractions...

CHAPTER ONE

੨

THE JUNGLE BOOK, 1967

Directed by Wolfgang Reitherman.
A Walt Disney animated feature adapted from Rudyard Kipling's stories.
The Jungle Book is a song-filled celebration of friendship, fun, and
adventure set in a lush and colorful world. Mowgli (Bruce Reitherman),
a boy raised by wolves, is befriended by a laid-back bear named Baloo
(Phil Harris) who joins him in his jungle adventures.

The Jungle Book, Disney's nineteenth animated masterpiece, was the last feature that Walt Disney personally supervised. He died after struggling with a suitable ending for his work, never seeing the completed feature. As Walt Disney's door closed with *The Jungle Book*, it opened a window to the bright new world that beckoned and awaited me.

There are certain wonders which you are never meant to know about or witness when you are a child. For example, wondering if your parents ever had sex... and if so, when? Or why the tooth fairy valued your friends' teeth more than yours. However, there is one wonder every child should experience and that is the spectacle of a family trip to the local cinema.

I grew up in South London with my older brother (four years, to be exact) and my parents, Richard and Kathryn. The local cinema was a dirty mecca where people came religiously to pray to the gods of film. No matter what time of the day you happened to drive past, a line of eager people would be forming (with no care of how bad the weather was), circumventing the dilapidated movie palace.

The old, balding ticket collector—affectionately referred to as "Stubby Knows" (for his vast film knowledge rather than a cruel comment in regards to his whiffer)—stood stationed

1

inside the large glass doors, always dressed proudly in his threadbare wine-colored suit. The tickets, boldly emblazoned with the words "ADMIT ONE," were taken from us by his yellowing, tobacco-stained fingers, and he would tear them carefully in half with precision and great care. Occasionally, he would catch a child's eager eyes and give his wise-with-age silent nod, as if rhythmically affirming some earlier prediction he had made.

Upon entering the shabby cinema, one would notice it was filled with wall-to-wall, untastefully matched red and gold furnishings, which at one time were an impressive gateway to a luxurious world. They were now but a pale impression of what they once were. Just a bit dirty, and downright manky, really. Lush thick-stained and worn carpets, red velvet seats (torn), and huge curtains which had obviously provided many a good meal for the moths rose high into the sky as far as the eye could see. They always left me pondering which lucky launderette got the chance to clean these cinematic beauties.

This theatrical splendor was situated very conveniently a short car journey away from home on the outskirts of Croydon. The cinema would soon become a second home to me, containing and witnessing within its walls most of the major events that would shape and influence me throughout my life. Going to the movies became an all-around great event and guaranteed, *won't-ever-let-you-down* fun for the weekend. A unique form of entertainment that had the power to capture the imaginations of the young and old attending the meticulously timed shows.

My earliest recollection of the fascinating culture of dimly lit rooms and enough sugar to send you into hyperactive convulsions was Disney's masterpiece *The Jungle Book*. It was a film that managed to magically transform my brother from a reserved seven-year-old into a singing, tree-swinging baboon for the subsequent journey home in the car.

When the lights gently dimmed and the curtains began to magically rise with a dull, mechanical whirl, the audience gradually grew silent as if wired to the same mechanism. This would be the start of my first feature film. My focus was initially pulled away from the massive white screen directly in front of me to the bright projection light at the very back of the cinema. While looking back into the magical, translucent cone, I scouted people's exhilarated reactions from behind me. The flickering light was like a shimmering jewel dancing within the flecks of dust that caught its attention, and the audience was suddenly transfixed by the story it had to tell. The din of the crowd now had diminished to an occasional whisper, and even that was quickly hushed by already-silent patrons as the previews for coming attractions rolled out before them. Each person stared directly ahead as if hypnotized, chewing their cinematic entrées at a steadily declining pace like a tin toy in desperate need of winding.

There are certain foods that became unique to the whole cinema experience. At the forefront of that category, of course, was popcorn. This was as American as we could get in Croydon. You would never eat it anywhere else other than within these walls—you just wouldn't suddenly start to crave it during the normal day. You just didn't, but as soon as you entered the cinema there was nothing else you wanted more. I would press my face against the warm glass of the counter in which the popcorn popped like a mutating organism, begging to be consumed. This unique taste would become a must-have for all young movie-going palates.

Then there were ice creams, lollypops, choc-ices, or the elusive *Cornetto*—the Italian ice cream of champions. A vanilla, chocolate-drizzled dream sprinkled with an assortment of nuts, served in a delicate sugar wafer with a frozen strawberry tip that refreshingly cleansed the palate as the last of the ice cream disappeared. This heavenly ice cream was not made in Italy as the deceptive name and commercials would suggest, but instead somewhere in the North of England. Along with its deceit it also carried a price that most parents alas could never afford. But these treats all suddenly became acceptable to eat even in the coldest winter, as long as they were consumed within the safety of the velvety cinema walls. You could step in from standing in a line for half an hour in the biting snow and head straight for the ice cream counter and it was okay. As your face rapidly defrosted in the tropical heat of the cinema's inner sanctum, the senses were ignited in excited preparation for the feature.

Along with the standard ice cream and popcorn came extraordinary bags of sweets. They were a dentist's worst nightmare, like props from the *Land of the Giants*, only available in such large sizes thanks to the Odeon cinema chain, all perfectly displayed in front of us. In your day-to-day life you could live happily on a normal pack of Opal Fruits, Maltesers, or a Mars Bar, but in the cinema you needed a wheelbarrow to cart away the king size, jumbo, Henry VIII, fat-bastard packs, sold for gluttonous consumption. The Odeon cinema lobby was like walking into Willy Wonka's factory on a weekly basis. And fuck the golden tickets—we had tatty, yellow paper tickets given to us by Stubby Knows upon our arrival to hastily grant us entry.

My older brother was a weaselly boy named Cymon (pronounced Simon, just spelled wanky to give him some added torment in school), and for as long as memory serves, we have loathed one another. It really isn't a personal thing. Eventually in life we would both search for some sort of rationale or interpretation for our dislike of one another, but our loathing was a hereditary thing: unlearned and mysterious, but always there. The only pleasure we really enjoyed and shared was when we went a few rounds of punching each other, or practicing various inventive methods of torture.

Normally, Cymon was a quiet child, but upon entering the cinema he would become a persistent whiner. He would trail my mother around like a shadow, with his precious torn yellow ticket stub firmly in his hand, whining and bringing her into a frantic argumentative state in which she would agree to most things (almost even a *Cornetto* ice cream) to make him cease. After making the mistake of reasoning with us about not eating a ridiculously expensive ice cream, her pride made it hopeless for her to argue her point from a monetary angle ever again. So, we would end up with the most that her limited funds could provide.

To me, being in a room where the lights slowly dimmed was a sure sign it was my bedtime. All that was missing were my father's gentle words "come on tupney, time for bediebyes." Within minutes of the commencement of *The Jungle Book* feature presentation, I took it upon myself to add my asthmatic snoring to the insanely joyful Disney soundtrack.

As the murmur and chatter of one hundred tiny critics gently awakened me from the warmth of the five layers of clothes piled on me to protect me from the winter's night outside, my reserved brother was nowhere to be found.

The mass doses of sugar, together with the hallucinogenic flickering lights, had suddenly given him passion. It was all, mind you, due to a dancing bear with coconut lips wearing a grass skirt, a singing, transfixing snake, and a young boy with no nipples, but it was genuine passion and excitement that Cymon so very rarely showed to the outside world, instead keeping it locked away and hidden deep inside. Of course, it was hard for me to share the same passion having only witnessed the opening screen and end credits rolling up. Sure they were nice credits but certainly not worthy of me strapping on my coconut lips and certainly nothing to scream and dance hysterically about. Normally, I would find myself glaring at my brother, seeing from him no empathy or camaraderie, only a cold revulsion, but for that one night he was totally and utterly alive and I truly loved him for it. My knees shook and I felt my grin unfurl from ear to ear at his tone and volume. I bit my lip to keep from laughing under the ecstasy of the entertaining power he had over us all as we watched him, the sparkle from the flickering projector still reflecting off him into my wide-with-wonder eyes.

I wanted to share this thing that could transform people; I wanted his movements, now quick and bold and sure and light. Everything about him flushed with gaiety and energy, and erupted in short Tourette's-like bouts of rapturous Disney song.

My parents would soon learn that the investment of a negligible ticket price returned a wealth of passionate emotions from us. So the local cinema soon became a frequent weekend event for our family, something we could all share and have an opinion on. I always loved to feel like grown-ups were truly interested in what I had to say, and with film we all saw different things and shared in each other's knowledge, likes and dislikes. This event was something where there truly was no right or wrong, just personal opinion, and age was suddenly and unequivocally irrelevant. It was a unique family occurrence that soon became greatly cherished and frequently attended by us all.

CHAPTER TWO

~~

GREASE, 1978

Directed by Randal Kleiser.
Energetic, imaginative film version of the long-running Broadway show about high-school life in the fifties. Danny (John Travolta), leader of the T-Bird gang, meets Sandy (Olivia Newton-John), his Aussie love interest, during the summer holiday. To his surprise, when Rydell High is back in session, Sandy is a new student there. She doesn't fit in with the cool crowd and sets out to change her image so she can win back her man. Hit songs include "Summer Nights" and "You're the One That I Want."

The now-frequent jaunt into Croydon with my family consisted of a forty-minute bumpy ride on bus number 68, taking us from one dirty street to another. The bus would conveniently drop us within walking distance of the closest cinema, right in the heart of the entertainment mecca commonly known as South London. Having traveled a total of an hour and twenty minutes to go *anywhere*, one would assume the destination worthy of such a trek. In Croydon this definitely was not the case. The streets were lined with filth, the people were bitter and miserable, and a fantastic night out meant a large kebab rather than the regular size, which, of course, went hand-in-hand proportionally with the amount you would subsequently vomit later that evening.

The arduous travel time for the passengers on the 68 bus inevitably reasserted how much they needed to escape the confines of the area in which they were born. Eighty minutes there and back if they were lucky—four thousand, eight hundred seconds reserved for personal reflection as the endless same-style Victorian houses passed slowly by on either side of the bus. Croydon was proud of touting the fact that it was the used car capital of the world, claiming that there was "a dealer on every corner." It was sad brag by any standards, but we clung to anything positive that we could find, no matter how small or ridiculous the claim. The area would gain some notoriety later in my life, entering England's consciousness by coining the slang term Croydon Facelift. This derogatory phrase referred to the working class hairstyle each girl in the area proudly displayed. The bleached ponytails were pulled back so tightly that their wearers' skin became taut, therefore ultimately saving Croydon women a bundle on cosmetic surgery. It was *that* type of town, inhabited by *those* types of people, living *that* type of crap life.

The section of South London in which I lived had the auspicious name of Thornton Heath, which actually sounds a lot nicer than the dirty hellhole that it was. I have no idea who or what Thornton was and there was definitely no Heath to be found there, so the name as a whole was deceiving. Then again, there were vast quantities of deceptive people who lived there, so I suppose in a peculiar sort of way the name fit the area perfectly.

For a bright-eyed six-year-old, though, a forty-minute bus ride into the main part of Croydon was actually quite thrilling, even something to look forward to. The double-decker red bus was the modern version of a horse-drawn carriage ride to the movie palace's ornate front doors. My mother would never let us sit on the top deck of the bus, pulling us quickly past the staircase that greeted us as we joyously bounded on. This was due to her own extreme fear of heights rather than out of concern for our safety. Our regular seat was the large, red, fuzzy, easily-accessible bench at the back of the bus reserved specifically for the elderly or disabled patrons. I'm not quite sure which of us fell into what category, or if we somehow managed to cover them all, but we were never moved on by the bus conductors, even though it riddled me with a strange sense of danger and excitement each time a fare collector would make his rounds plodding lethargically past us.

On one such particular journey, I focused my attention on my brother's eyes for any kind of sign of the adventure that might lay before us that night; a twinkle, even a slight hint of glistening like the one he had recently exhibited after *The Jungle Book* experience while he sat perched on the opposite side of the bus from me. He was far enough away so as not to be associated with me in the slightest, but still, of course, within my mother's firm, easy grasp. But alas, the dancing light, the gift he had taken away from our last trip to the cinema, was most definitely absent. It had been replaced with his regular boredom, deep thoughts, and an inherent sullenness that he strangely felt burdened with for such a young lad. The excitement was not emanating from my wanky brother in the *slightest* on this occasion, but my mother seemed a little more fruity than normal, in retrospect. As we were bobbed around by the jerky bus movements, she suddenly seemed as close to us in age as she ever had before that night. Energy and excitement emanated from her every fluid movement.

"Why isn't daddy coming?" I asked, cutting the silence as potholes in the street jolted the bus.

"Dad is too busy to come, darling," she quickly replied, not even feigning to believe her own lie.

My mother lifted me high in her arms so I could pull on the cord that in turn would signal the driver to stop the bus outside the cinema. A muffled bell could be heard toward the front of the carriage, filling me with a strange sense of power, and in turn ringing in the commencement of the night's fun. Upon arrival at our destination we passed Stubby, the old ticket-ripper, who also exhibited a great deal more life and enthusiasm than normal while standing guard at his now-familiar post. He commented on my brightly colored abundance of winter attire as I entered and handed him a fistful of yellow tickets. The added attention from Stubby made my night, as I was a sucker for any grown-up who showed interest in or asked any questions of me whatsoever.

I watched Stubby, intrigued by his demeanor, instead of taking my usual post at the sweet counter (where I would only be verifying the arrangement of syrupy delights which I had set to memory anyway). With his hands held firmly behind his back, Stubby bounced rhythmically on the balls of his feet. He occasionally let out a few notes of an undisclosed tune, humming in short bursts, before he would catch himself and return to his solitary standing. His eyes darted to either side to see if his crime had been witnessed by any of the tiny observers or their guardians. What on earth was going on here?

The poster for the evening's feature proclaimed *"Grease is the word. Grease is the way we are feeling,"* but instead, to me the word was *naptime,* and the way I was feeling was absolutely knackered after my seemingly endless journey. The doors to a whole new cinematic genre were about to open for me: The Musical. It was a genre packed full of gay explosions of color and song and dance, which, ironically for adults, is enjoyed mostly by gay men dressed flamboyantly in explosions of color with a love for shimmy.

The John Travolta, Olivia Newton-John dance spectacular *Grease,* full of 1950's tarts of both the male and female variety who burst into a tune for no particular reason at all, was an utter revelation to me. An epiphany of sorts. It was absolutely fantastic, and absolutely, unequivocally American.

Once inside the inner sanctum of the cinema my mother's excitement escalated to a full-on tizzy at the very mention of John Travolta, and it transformed her children into something completely new… a great *excuse* for her to be away from the reality of her husband for an evening. As she watched her idol shake his hips on the screen, hand jiving at the slightest of opportunities, the excitement overcame her. My mother was filled from her toes to her face with a sudden burst of energy, and by the end of the movie it had sent her quite literally dancing into the aisles.

When you are young enough, there is no such thing as shame or embarrassment or coyness. It seemed perfectly normal and fun for me watching my mother's impromptu dance performance to the amusement of all surrounding her. I really did try and put up a brave fight to stay awake for the film in its entirety; I too wanted to share the excitement my brother and now my mother had felt on a trip to this magical cinematic room, but yet again, it was to no avail.

For me, the whole *Grease* experience consisted of the trailers for other movies I could sleep through at a later date, and then ten minutes of the main attraction before I felt the weight of my eyelids bearing down as if delicately fashioned from lead. I had made it quickly through an entire king-size Mars Bar during the trailers, and I wasn't going down this time without a fight. My tiny fingers held my eyelids wide open, but it was no use; as soon as a cramp set into my pudgy arm, the game was all but over. The battle to stay awake and witness movie magic was lost once more. I felt a definite, annoying sleep pattern emerging here.

12

Strangely enough, the only time I drifted in and out of the movie was at the very end scene where Olivia Newton-John bopped and danced around in her black, skin-tight, hip-hugging, silky hot pants. Looking back I have often thought this was no coincidence. Far from it. This was obviously a gift to me from the god of movies. I truly believe this. Why not? He has shown himself before throughout the pages of history in times of need. Just read the Bible—it's all written down in black and white. It's very well documented that God's son was brought gifts at a very early age when the messiah was quite needy himself. He was the recipient of gold, frankincense, and myrrh as he lay sleeping, probably trying to keep himself awake for the main feature, no doubt. What the hell is myyyrrrrrrrhhhh anyway? Mary and Joseph must have been a little pissed off at the presentation of a large vat of myyyyrrrrrrrrrrrrhhhhhh. They probably would have preferred something else I'm sure, an upgrade in their accommodations at the very least would have been handier, but instead the lucky parents of the messiah were presented with "mmmmmyyyyyyrrrrrrrrrrrrrrrrrrrrrrhhhh." Exactly how *wise* could these men have been bringing forth such a crap gift? Or maybe they just didn't have a lot of time to shop, it was kind of last minute with the whole proclamation thing after all, so mmmmyyyrrrrrrrrrhhhhh it was.

You can just imagine Mary and Joseph looking frantically over the myrrh once the wise men had left to see if there was still a price label on it so they could return it to the shop.

"Oh...thank you very much...and what exactly do you use this for again?"

"It's the thought that counts, Joseph. We could always pass it off and give it as a gift to someone else next Christmas."

13

"Yeah, I suppose so darling… What's Christmas?"

That tradition of the useless gift at Christmas that you really could have done without was created on that very day and was proudly carried on by my flatulent grandmother, who provided us with a whole range of myrrh-type gifts throughout her declining senile years. There's always one in the family, isn't there?

But I digress. The god of movies, who had always been kind to me, on this day brought forth a very special gift—a lasting impression of everything I would ever want in a woman, etched into my fragile six-year-old mind to be retrieved at a later date. The movie goddess Olivia Newton-John in all her dancing and singing glory, otherwise known as innocent, soon-to-be-transformed Sandy. She had strands of gold in her hair and long, beautiful legs (which probably smelled like frankincense); most importantly, she had access to a full-scale, top-notch fun fair. Wow, that's my girl.

I've often thought that if I were ever to go on the quiz show *Mastermind*, my specialist subjects would be "Movie Openings" and "End Titles." I probably couldn't recognize the film in its entirety except for the first and last few minutes, which I could recall with absolute confidence. This dodgy pattern of watching films was going to have to change. I loved them for the time I was lucky enough to be awake, but staying awake was proving to be a major hurdle. My thinking cap would have to replace the ridiculous woolen bobble hat I currently wore on outings to the cinema.

My father had chosen to sit this musical film experience out. It's not that he had absolutely no interest in the film, or that he was a jealous man in regard to my mother's Travolta infatuation; in fact, to his credit he was quite the opposite. He just wanted to give my mother a night to live in another world with the dancing Mr. Travolta, without the reality of her husband sitting next to her, we would later come to discover. He was already well aware of the power of cinema, the enjoyment and the subsequent transportation to other worlds it could bring to the open onlookers. This kind of movie was not really his *thing*, but it was most definitely a big *thing* for my mother, so why would he diminish it in any kind of way? I slept soundly opposite my brother, my head placed gently in my mother's lap for the entire bus ride home after the film's and my mother's dance-spectacular finale. The only sound echoing in my ears was a lullaby hummed by my mother, a soft and gentle song as she delicately stroked my golden, wispy hair... *It's a real pussy wagon—Greased Lightning! Oh oh oh ooooooooo...*

Thank you, Mr. Travolta.

CHAPTER THREE

ॐ

THE GOLDEN VOYAGE OF SINBAD, 1974

Directed by Gordon Hessler.
A delightful rehash of earlier Sinbad adventures that evokes memories of
Saturday matinees in the 1950s. A display of Ray Harryhausen's finest
dynamation effects including a six-armed statue that sword-battles with
Sinbad (John Phillip Law), an enraged cyclops centaur, and a winged
griffin. Sinbad takes on the evil sorcerer Koura (Tom Baker), who is
out to get Sinbad's golden talisman to complete a spell.

Musicals proved not to be my father's thing, but a fantasy-action-adventure film would definitely spark both his and my vivid imaginations, respectively. *The Golden Voyage of Sinbad* (*Sinbad*, for short) proved to be the perfect candidate. It was a movie we had been enticed to see by way of endless television teaser-trailers. We were both easily sold on the idea, transfixed by the images like a snake by his charmer.

I was at the awkward kind of age where I still wasn't old enough to go to the cinema by myself but didn't want to act too much like a child, of course. Stubby, at this juncture, had acquired a new cinematic accomplice: the statuesque blonde ticket seller, Michelle. Her name was proudly emblazoned onto an Odeon cinema name tag for the long queue of customers to read. She actually could have been there all along, but to me she now made herself most visible. Michelle showered me with attention that in turn made me uncomfortable. "He's so adorable," she would now weekly proclaim, "look at those cheeks!" Her voice instantly transformed into a high squawk as her eyes thinned into a squint peering down at me. Michelle never actually conversed with me, but instead would comment as an aside to my father as if I was an adorable imbecile, clueless to what her word formations meant. What was so abnormal about my cheeks? My father, thankfully, proved a very willing chaperone to our action-adventure quest, holding my hand tighter as we inched within reading distance of Michelle's name tag at the ticket counter.

Unfamiliar adults as a whole made me nervous, due mainly to the infrequent introductions to anyone or anything gained from my very limited surroundings. My world still basically consisted of the confines of my home and the few encompassing streets I was allowed to venture onto, mapped out methodically by my mother. I didn't dare cross the borders she had designated, as it would undoubtedly have unleashed her terrifying inner dragon, a monster far beyond even Sinbad's expertise. Instead, I would stand on the furthest allowable curb, peering across to the outlawed roads with curiosity and wonder. For all I knew, the sword-fighting creatures and gladiators I was soon to witness in *Sinbad* could have been filmed on those forbidden streets. There had to be some good reason for my mother's stringent rules, after all.

My mother was undoubtedly the family disciplinarian, cartographer, and general lawmaker, but for this particular cinematic outing, my father had temporarily assumed her place at the helm. He expertly steered our *Sinbad* adventure on the high seas like an old sea dog, as our proverbial ship docked once more at the exotic doors of the Odeon cinema in Croydon, joining the queue of other eager adventurers and their chaperones.

My father's wealth of knowledge went far beyond the quickest route to the local cinema, I would inevitably discover. He was like a great set of encyclopedia volumes, unobtrusive with a distinct, familiar smell, and always close at hand for me.

With age he had become a little worn around the edges, but was brimming with information if ever anyone took the trouble to inquire. A mention of the movie *The Jungle Book* could spark a conversation on Rudyard Kipling and his collected works. *Sinbad*, I soon discovered, might spark a diatribe on Greek mythology, and so it went.

Any question you wanted answered, or dared to ask, he would inevitably have the answer to. His answer was always plain and simple, without a pause or hesitation crossing the lines and furrows of his face, enlightening an eager seven-year-old child with his adult wisdom. His soft tones were never patronizing, and he never spoke to me as the ticket seller did, as if I were an imbecile. I was instead always his *little learning man*, which to this day, I still remain. He would take time to sit me down at the table and talk, comfort, or find help and solutions for my homework or troubles. He patiently encouraged me to write my first words. He would place his hands carefully over mine, his rough from labor and cracking with age, and guide mine through each letter until my unsure motions took on their own bold energy. His indelible imprint was left with me for the rest of my days. Never again would I be able to pick up a pen without literally having him in the form and body of every one of my words.

The one thing my brother and I loved my father for—and my mother constantly tormented him about—was the fact that he didn't have a disciplined regimen with us. His parents, Marie and Phillip, both bred from a military background, had showered upon him an abundance of physical torment, including lashings with a cane and mouth scrubbings with industrial detergent to cleanse away the filth that, to their ears, he supposedly uttered. As my father himself had yet to see the profit of this sort of punishment, he had chosen not to pass on the troubling family legacy. My brother and I, of course, were most grateful at the breaking of this destructive cycle, and in turn did our best to not let his kindness go unnoticed or unappreciated.

I skipped with my father hand in hand to the movie theater that afternoon filled with anticipation and brimming with excitement. I was not to be disappointed. This manifestation of the hero, Sinbad, and his cunning band of monsters was absolutely incredible. However, it was to me a scary movie whichever way I looked at it. Sure, scary movies were no new thing to me. I'd seen other really harrowing films at this point—*101 Dalmations, The Rescuers, Bambi,* and *The Fox and the Hound*— not only linked by great McDonald's Happy Meal toys but also in the effect each film had on my nervous system. But these were Disney cartoons, and therefore had to be taken with a large grain of Disney pixie dust. In *Sinbad* I saw real-life walking skeletons, a six-armed fighting goddess, and a plethora of bizarre, breathing, utterly shifty monsters courtesy of Ray Harryhausen's mastery of special effects.

My grandmother was not only a harsh woman but also— adding to the confusion and panic of her ominous presence—a master of speaking in cryptic phrases, half-finished sentences, and bizarre old wives' tales. She had taken sheer joy in telling me, "If you don't eat your greens your hair won't get curly." Ironically this myth, to this day, is still the sole reason why I don't eat vegetables. (An Afro is about the furthest thing from any of my wish lists.) In addition to this strange promise, she had also instilled into me the saying, "The camera never lies." Thus, using her twisted, senile logic, I concluded that the monsters I witnessed in *Sinbad* must be real, and surely all inhabited my bedroom wardrobe. I was convinced that when the lights were extinguished, they were all undoubtedly feasting on the greens I refused to eat from her plates, all adorned with perfectly coiffed Afros.

Movie-going was ever changing, due only in part to the discovery of Michelle. Obsessive-compulsive routines and seemingly endless lists of pointless film trivia were now being stored in my fragile young brain. I had entered the magical domain of the cinema walls enough times at this point to have made some priceless discoveries about my Saturday afternoon movie rituals, which I will gladly list here:

1. Eat enough sugar, and stay awake for the entire film.

2. Arrive early to the cinema. It was *essential* to see the coming attractions, otherwise known as *future tomfoolery*.

3. Buy ANY souvenir program or film-related, useless crap they were offering at the concession stand.

4. Beware of the snap-down chair. It was the final, ruthless guardian of the sacred cinema.

5. Force yourself to go to the bathroom *before* the film commences. Otherwise, you were bound to miss the most incredible special effect in the movie, without doubt the scene your friends had been talking about for weeks. In terms of school playground etiquette, you would have to lie about having seen it.

Sharing your weekend movie jaunts at school was now a huge part of the whole cinematic experience. Not only did you see the film for personal entertainment's sake, you saw films like *Sinbad* so you could share the excitement and fun on a dull Monday morning. If any genre of movie would get us all talking at Cypress Infant School, adventure movies were in a league of their own. It was without-a-doubt the action-packed extravaganzas we all adored and all clammored to see as soon as they were released.

Thomas Burns was the Cypress Infant School playground master of movie plots and storyline twists. He was the South London schoolboy shaman, claiming his throne early on in the game. He had two major claims to fame:

1. His grandma (obviously not as insane as mine) had survived the *Titanic* disaster as a child, which we thought was pretty intriguing, of course.

2. Any movie you might happen to mention you wanted to see, even if the release date was years away, he would certainly have already seen it. Guaranteed.

The boy was a master of imagination; he was the equivalent of Norris McWhirter in terms of *useless fucking movie trivia*. You could never catch him out. He said he had seen everything from the *Texas Chainsaw Massacre,* which we didn't even want to question him on, to *Sinbad,* which he had witnessed weeks ago. Due to the fact I had seen the film with my father on its opening weekend, I naturally found it necessary to question him on the location of his obvious advanced screening. "I've seen so many clips from the film on the television that they have all joined together forming the complete motion picture," he replied in a tone shocked at my audacity to even think to question the movie master. He did not hesitate or show any degree of being even slightly flustered.

21

Now this was a top rate answer from the fella. The only bits of the movie we could ever question him on up to the film's release were the clips that we had all seen on television anyway, so to this day he could never have been proved a liar and continued on in school legend as our walking encyclopedia on film facts and pointless trivia. In my quiet adult times of peacefulness, when I am in the place just before my dream state, when I am relaxed and at ease with myself and the world, I find myself quietly thinking, "What was the name of the clockwork owl in *Clash of the Titans?*" or "What was the evil sorcerer's name in *Sinbad?*"

Aaarrrrhhhhh. Bloody Hell.

I still find myself thinking up questions about bloody *Sinbad* and other action-adventure films just in case I was to run into Thomas Burns again, so I could at last catch out the self-proclaimed, pathologically lying trivia king. In hindsight I missed the most important, dead-giveaway sign about Thomas Burns' reliability: His eyebrows were completely joined. He was a uni-brow, a so-called furry forehead. A sure sign that this half-werewolf, half-boy meant he could not be bloody trusted with his trivia anyway... unless, of course, it was about *American Werewolf in London,* to which I'm quite sure he would have had a whole host of insider knowledge!

As young film critics, we thought we had reached a crescendo with *Sinbad.* What other magical world could there be to shadow such a masterpiece? It didn't take long for our question to be answered.

CHAPTER FOUR

STAR WARS EPISODE IV: A NEW HOPE, 1977

Directed by George Lucas.
Elaborate update of the immortal battle between good and evil that would later become one of the most popular films of all time. A young man, Luke Skywalker (Mark Hamill), becomes an interplanetary hero with the help of some human and robot friends. Accolades include Academy Awards for various technical achievements and John Williams' rousing score. The first film in a trilogy followed by Episode V: The Empire Strikes Back *and* Episode VI: Return of the Jedi.

Undoubtedly, the Star Wars Trilogy would be in my top five best-of-the-best movie list. To separate the movies from one another would be virtually impossible for any and every schoolboy. Why? For precisely two reasons:

1. Because the movies would take up more than half of the top five and that would just be... silly.

2. Because the movies became such a cultural part of my generation, influencing every viewer's adolescence in such a way that splitting them would just be... wrong.

It was very difficult for me to watch a black-and-white movie as a child. They were just rather *dull* in every sense of the word. Movies were a way for me to escape into different galaxies and adventures. Nowhere in my wildest dreams did I ever want to enter a black-and-white universe; it would have completely shattered the whole fantasy aspect. To this day, a B/W film to me means Before the Wars. *Star Wars*, that is. I know now, of course, that there were some classics made

Before the Wars; it's just that they didn't really interest me back then. Much more importantly, though, they didn't have sodding great merchandise that good old George Lucas had the genius to provide every willing child with.

I saw the original film with my entire family at Croydon's Whitgift Shopping Centre in a newly opened cinema, giving some much needed competition to Stubby's monopoly. It became a new mecca for children on the weekends with two great added bonuses. Depending on which cinema door you exited from, the gateway led directly out into either:

1. The golden arches. A McDonald's slap-bang right in front of your eyes and stomach. The providers of a Happy Meal—and shortly after its consumption, a not-so-happy toilet.

2. A gargantuan toy store containing almost any toy conceivable in a child's imagination.

What an absolutely great marketing strategy by the owners of these kid-friendly stores. This was my introduction to a whole different side of the cinema. Even after the first *Star Wars* movie debuted in England, merchandise was still pretty scarce. Maybe a badge or a sticker, a toy blaster or a couple of action figures. ACTION FIGURES, not dolls! Let's make that crystal clear; there's a BIG difference. Up until this point nobody could predict the impact this film would have on society, or maybe nobody really understood how powerful George Lucas's Jedi mind control was. I came away on that life-altering day with an orange R2-D2 badge bought from the concession stand and a Princess Leia *Star Wars* paper drinking cup, and still felt I'd come out a winner. Granted, it was no plastic Millennium Falcon, with detachable roof and access via the gun turret, but these merchandise wonders were being hurriedly developed for a later toy onslaught. Nevertheless, the orange badge and paper cup were a start to my own *Star Wars* universe. How little I knew or could possibly comprehend about the glorious field of film tie-in toys that lay glistening before me, softly calling to me from the shelves—"Buy me…buy me…you won't regret it…I'll be a good action figure; I promise I'll win every battle for you…"

I was a boy who truly believed he was at this age a man. As I write this now it strikes me as rather poignant, as I see that my Jedi circle is now complete. I am now a man who truly believes he is still a mere boy. Wanting to grow up fast, as all kids do, was not so I could go to work, smoke fags, drive, drink, or have children of my own—far from it. I needed the years to pass me by quickly so I could see how the sodding *Star Wars* trilogy would end. We all prodded Thomas Burns for story line answers, but even he seemed hard-pressed to explain the trilogy's finale.

I will never forget the sinking feeling every child experienced in the pit of their stomachs upon leaving *The Empire Strikes Back*, knowing we still had another two to three years before *Return of the Jedi* was released. Luke had lost his hand, Darth Vader had a cabbage for a head, and Han Solo had been frozen in some dodgy black material. Could it get any worse? How could this hopeless, venturesome situation possibly turn around, George Lucas? Would it be like an episode of a fifties serial, such as *The Lone Ranger* or *Buck Rogers*, where a seemingly desperate and deadly situation could all be magically solved in the next thrilling installment? Maybe Han Solo didn't really go into the dodgy frozen black stuff? Maybe we would find him dining casually on a feast of Vader cabbage-head with a nice Bordeaux being held by Luke's detachable hand when the next movie began? Only time would tell, but it felt like the end of the world for my friends and me. To help pass the time and ease my pain, our friend George Lucas began to fill, and I mean fill, the local shops with a huge assortment of merchandise so we could fight our own toy battles. We could in the meantime conjure up our own destinies for our beloved characters. Merchandise. What I wouldn't do for a great piece of *Star Wars* merchandise! To what lengths would I go? I was soon about to find out.

It was Christmas 1977, and our local department store Allders was offering a themed yuletide trip into Santa's Grotto, proudly featuring *Star Wars* characters and toys as some of the give-away gifts at the conclusion of the grotto grab-fest. That was all the information I needed to hear; I was there, ready to join the faithful in line. As luck would have it, so were about three hundred other children, dragging their parents with them, joining a line that looped the circumference of the entire store as far as the eye could see. The concept of a Christmas Grotto was always kind of scary to me, and as I soon found out via the film A *Christmas Story*, completely the same the world over. The thought of plodding slowly in crocodile formation down dark tunnels filled with Santa's little helpers so an old fat man with a fake beard, rosacea, and pickled onion breath could sit you on his knee was, to say the least, a little strange.

I finally reached good old elephantine Santa, used my few seconds with him wisely, relayed swiftly the list of *Star Wars* merchandise that I wanted, and was moved quickly on through the production line. As a final farewell upon departing Santa's intergalactic planet, I was presented with a wrapped Christmas package by one of Santa's little Jawa helpers, tinsel draped to make the character not look so threatening and *Star Wars* related. After all, this wasn't the Jawa's desert of Tantoinee; this was the cold plains of Lap-Land, where Santa was the reigning emperor. Could this truly magical old man, draped in a red velvet cloak, surrounded by his forces, really have deciphered with his sorcery what I wanted for Christmas?

Of course he could! I had just told him to his red face.

I gladly snatched the package and unwrapped it feverishly…what on my wish list would this joyous old man be granting? Would it be a twelve-inch Darth Vader with detachable cloak and light saber? A Chewbacca warrior belt which doubled as a complete carrying case for all my *Star Wars* figurines? An extending, glowing, Obi-Wan light saber I could clobber my brother with?

But no, the magic man, otherwise known as Father Fat Christmas, had come through and answered every boy's wish instead with… a pink squeaky teething toy for dogs. Oh, great, thank you O'bearded wise one! Was he having a laugh? I had subjected myself to hours' worth of badly sung Christmas carols by Jawas, a whole host of imbeciles, and a fat old man in a dodgy mince-pie encrusted beard for a squeaky dog toy? I was completely and utterly devastated, but I had one great weapon up my sleeve that the givers of such a crap gift had seemingly forgotten about—**THE FORCE**. The influence of a depressed, whiny kid, one of the most powerful forces in any universe. Maybe my dad could sort something out for me? I needed the *Father Force* to sort out sodding *Father Christmas*. I think that my dad himself was a little upset at me. Not because we didn't even own a dog, but because I had subjected him to the stupid

Jawa grotto for over two hours. The poor man didn't even get to sit on pickled-onion-breath's knee and put forth his own wish list. It's no wonder he was upset, come to think of it. We headed home in complete silence, the festive spirit ripped from us both, unwilling for different reasons to make any sort of eye contact with one another. The silence of the drive was broken only by the occasional random *squeak* from the pink animal toy that lay delicately in my lap.

The department store, unbeknownst to them, had made one grave mistake. My dad was a journalist by trade, and a distressed child story searching out a happy ending is always print worthy. Especially when it was your child. In this twisted society, bad news is in fact the only real news worth reporting. Kids dying of leukemia or kids given a raw deal by fat corporations are practically one in the same when it comes to selling newspapers. That week a full page story appeared in the *Croydon Advertiser* with yours truly pictured in all his glory, my sad puppy eyes as the focal snapshot. A truly heart-melting story, and more importantly, of course, top news in South London. At last—fame within my school and circle of friends. All would hail to the king of the squeaky pink dog toy.

And then as if by Santa magic, a strange thing happened. The very same day the story appeared in the paper we received a phone call from the manager of Allders. The store, in its shame, invited me back as a guest of honor to the toy wonderland. I was allowed one toy, ANY TOY, free of charge as a sincere apology for the misery they had put me through. As an added bonus, a photographer was there to capture the happy moment and, of course, to cover Allders' bottom and save a little face.

I knew what I wanted instantly, but I tried my best to look overwhelmed and confused at the whole situation. I gently released myself from the clutch of my father's hand and began to search carefully through the shelves, knowing full-well already where my prize lay. I had touched it a hundred times, after all, in the previous months, and put every inch of its detail to memory. Smitten as I was with *Star Wars*, I was very nearly swayed by the most expensive item in the entire store. A motorized, miniature, metal army jeep big enough to sit comfortably in and do some damage on any kids' battlefield. Now *that's* a toy worth having. Heck, I could even drive myself to school in that little beauty. As I made a beeline for the jeep, the sales assistant saw his job flash before his eyes and masterfully diverted my path, redirecting me to the more sensibly priced "ANY TOY" items within the store. I turned the final aisle where Han Solo's pride and joy lay docked in its bay. No wonder that conniving Greedo was so eager to get his dirty hands on it. Princess Leia had ridiculed the Millennium Falcon upon viewing it for the first time. Without offending her highness, how very wrong the Princess was. It was a rescue ship, a way out for the Princess and the department store alike.

This was an absolute beauty in every sense of the word. Boxed, large enough to be cumbersome, but that was a bonus to my tiny hands. This felt like the gift to end all gifts. I would gladly carry it home in wobbly light-speed back to my own galaxy, not so far-far away. With one click of the photographer's camera and a silly overexcited grin on my face, finally the Millennium Falcon would be mine, and both the paper and I would have a happy ending. Oh yes. One happy nipper courtesy of what originally came in the form of a pink squeaky hammer a dog could chew on and a red-faced, fat, bearded Santa-wannabe employed by an embarrassed corporation.

Cheers. The Force is strong in this one. Happy Christmas.

CHAPTER FIVE

৯৯

THE WIZARD OF OZ, 1939

Directed by Victor Fleming.
A true American classic. Based on L. Frank Baum's story of Kansas girl
Dorothy Gale (Judy Garland) who is transported to the magical land of
Oz via tornado. Accompanied by a colorful cast of characters while being
chased by a Wicked Witch (Margaret Hamilton), Dorothy embarks on an
adventure to find a Wizard and her way home. Academy Award winner
for Best Song, "Over the Rainbow," and Herbert Stothart's score.
Garland also won a special miniature Oscar for her performance.

The Wizard of Oz is known in Great Britain as a television holiday movie. It could be Christmas, Easter, Mother's Day, Rubbish Men Day—any holiday for that matter—but it never really dawned on me how twisted the television schedulers were until my adult years. Just when kids were trying to wind down and relax from the stress and strain of day-to-day school life, just as they began to really tranquilize and enjoy their well-deserved holidays, along came the Wicked Witch of the West. To this day, pictures of Margaret Hamilton, who played the Wicked Witch, in or out of her Oz makeup, still scare me—there is just something inherently evil and unnerving about that woman's features.

Without fail, every Christmas evening after filling myself with twice my body weight in chocolate, stolen from various members of my family, I would put aside the Millennium Falcon and we would all sit down as a group to watch the timeless spectacle that was Oz, the land of the Emerald City. My brother soon became increasingly untrusting of me as the years progressed and caught on to my grandiose chocolate-stealing scheme, so he would periodically disappear after opening his sweets to hide them like a rabid sweet-toothed squirrel. He normally hid them in a vacant drawer in my parents' bedroom wardrobe, but as with everything else in the house, I knew exactly where to find his chocolates. This proved to be more of a pointless game than any kind of true obstacle for me in the obtainment of sugar.

Whenever I was unattended in the house, I went through each family member's personal possessions, and as a result, I had all rooms mapped out and burnt to memory, including all the best nooks and crannies in which to place things for safe-keeping or…stealing. Most of the time when rifling through other people's possessions I was not looking for anything specific, I was really just looking. A whole host of valuable personal articles were to be found in my parents' drawers, these being the most fun and carrying with them the greatest danger of capture and, consequently, the harshest punishment. I would make up elaborate stories of the history of the golden pocket watch lying at the bottom of my father's drawer, tracing the intricate engraving on it with my fingertip. My mother's hoard included inherited antique jewelry and crumpled, musty photographs, which I tried to match to one another. For each piece I handled I would in turn spend hours conjuring the historic timeline of how it made its way into my grubby little hands.

I would regularly thicken my wallet with my brother's stashed money—coins and paper. I had no preference as it really held little actual relevance to me. I would pack it until it became almost impossible to remove it from my pocket, and I would carry it with me proudly everywhere, as if I had earned every penny through backbreaking labor. I was a master pilferer by my own assessment, with my naturally angelic face being the biggest crime and deceit thus far. The Christmas holidays brought with them a new selection of presents waiting to be pinched from my brother's stash, but also the annual, more disturbing, *Wizard of Oz* tradition.

No movie villain has ever physically affected me as the Wicked Witch of the West did. The potent combination of the swift energy rush from the chocolate and the sheer terror of that green bitch riding her bike through thin air was enough to set my underpants on the rinse cycle—literally. The first number of times it happened, my family members found some strange cuteness in the urine puddle that lay on the floor as my eyes widened with terror. As the years traveled by, the humor seemed to evaporate rapidly, as did anyone in my vicinity, as the now-infamous transformation scene approached. She totally and utterly took over my mind—and bladder, her urine spell effectively cast. The Wicked Witch of the West was, at this juncture, the cause of many phobias and ridiculous reactions in my still innocent mind:

1. I had recurring nightmares that my schoolteachers all rode bikes with baskets and were called Ms. Gulch.

2. I panicked at the sound of bad weather in case of a sudden tornado. Due to the dreariness of the English climate this meant, of course, that I was spooked for a large portion of my childhood.

3. I couldn't leave my feet hanging over the end of the bed for fear that during the night the Witch would mistake me for Dorothy and make a grab for my new prized Kevin Keegan slippers.

Without a doubt, the most disturbing of all of my reactions was that I couldn't look my mother directly in the eye, due to her strange, ever-growing resemblance to the witch. I had questioned as a child why God had played such a cruel trick on her by giving her petite, beautiful face such a large, crooked nose. The kind of nasal trumpet Barry Manilow or Barbra Streisand would even stare at so they could have a laugh at someone else's proboscis. It was as if a new window of perception had been opened for me; this prominent attribute of hers suddenly became all too noticeable. From the first time I witnessed the movie, my mother seemed to develop the strange power of almost totally transforming herself into the Witch. You just expected there to be billowing red smoke and flames to punctuate the end of one of her many diatribes of rage, for the ground to suddenly open up and swallow her back into its depths. This was totally plausible, and while I cowered in her angered, larger-than-life shadow, it seemed quite probable.

My mother had developed this frustration and anger as a result of growing up with overbearing, adoptive parents, Donald and Nelly. Donald, at one time in his life a strapping young fireman, was now reduced to sitting in his maroon velvet chair, barely able to move—all but waiting to die, chain-smoking to help attain his goal. Because he was always annoyed at the noise my brother and I made, my grandmother constantly flitted around the house trying to smooth things over.

Upon entering it, their home was always rich with the smell of old people. It left a thick, pungent coating in the fibers of your clothes, like a little parting gift you had no desire for but were obliged to leave with anyway. They were much less benign in the days of my mother's childhood.

Reaching the age when adulthood beckoned, my mother began applying for jobs only to literally have my grandmother call the prospective employers to list for them the reasons why they shouldn't employ her daughter. Ridicule and shame in turn drew from my mother the little self-confidence she had, giving her a permanent melancholy demeanor. From then on she lived as if she were a beautiful, dying star always on the brink of burning out. My mother, much to her own disappointment, rebelled against her upbringing only to slip into a similar regimen of discipline with my brother and me. Perhaps that is why my mind likened her to the Wicked Witch? The petrifying image of my mother, now permanently embedded in the forefront of my mind, was made even more terrifying when she discovered that the local bully, Jason White, had chosen my brother as his new target of terror.

Jason White was the quintessential school bully. There must be some sort of bully finishing school that each local education authority is required to have a few chosen kids attend so they can be placed randomly throughout the educational system. Jason White had quite obviously excelled there. He was well below average in looks, underwhelming in intelligence, and constantly surrounded by a plethora of worshippers to help carry out his every command. He was like a little terrorizing Nazi with the essential shaved head and knee-high Dr. Martens boots. He carried a permanent scowl as if his pursed, thin lips trapped an angry bee inside his mouth that was searching aimlessly for an exit with its stinger.

He also adorned himself with a variety of earrings randomly placed throughout his left earlobe. Only in one ear— the left, of course—otherwise it was a known playground fact that you were gay. Having your left ear pierced meant you would likely be roughhousing with the hooligan supporters of the local football team. A piercing in the right or, God forbid, *both* ears meant you were fighting for the supporters of the local pink team. We didn't make the rules, we just followed them—to a tee. Jason would routinely carve the racist white supremacy National Front logo on various stationary objects or write some ingenious profanity on anyone or anything that dared come too close to him. There are some children in society who just need to go directly to *prison college* to prepare them for their inevitable life. Jason White was Cypress Junior School's primary candidate for such a nomination.

Do not pass "Go."

Do not collect two hundred pounds.

No "get out of jail" free card for him. PLEASE.

The arduous daily journey home from school became sadly routine. Jason White had convinced himself and, more importantly, his band of moronic brothers that stepping in what can only be described as fresh, steaming *dog shit* was good luck. Obviously, and quite logically, it must not have been good luck for him to go home to his mother with this charm still attached to the bottom of his school shoes, so my brother's clean-pressed trousers became Jason's nightly wiping post, much to Cymon's dismay. This malodorous pattern continued for weeks. School bell rings. Kids pile out of classrooms. My brother and I walk home. He gets some crap wiped on his leg, and then to top off his beautiful day, my mother verbally vomits on him for letting it happen AGAIN, as if this was something he enjoyed and encouraged Jason to do. Of course, Mum— thanks for your help and logic. Why *wouldn't* Cymon want some crap on his leg?

It was week three of this tragically familiar cycle. Eleven shit days at school had passed, followed by eleven equally shit nights for my brother. Catching us all quite unawares one day while walking home, showered by a light rain, my mum appeared magically as if propelled upward from the earth's core in all of her raging glory. Being already spooked myself and on tornado watch at this point, this vision did nothing to ease my anguish. Wanting to interrupt the cycle that had now become so commonplace, she scooped up the infamous bully with one hand, lifting him high off the ground with that special kind of bizarre mother strength. Jason, much to everyone's surprise, let out a pathetic yelp, a sound as though a puppy had been accidentally stepped on.

"You think dog shit's funny, do you, my little pretty?" my mother frighteningly cackled.

In a moment of complete confusion, and with Jason's lucky charm still attached to his foot, Mum looked at him, staring directly into his beady, cold eyes, and shockingly, he looked right back at her, directly into her relentless stare. Maybe it's not as brave as it sounds on his part because he really had no choice in the matter, as his head was locked in position by her arm, but witnessing Jason taking the full impact of her sharp, piercing words at point-blank range seemed a terrifying scenario to the rest of us.

"Do you know who I am?" she continued screaming at Jason.

Is this some sort of trick question? I pondered as I looked upon the terrible scene with the school bully. Did she mean *Do you know who I am...apart from an obviously insane mother?*

"I am a witch, and unless this shit stops, I will cast an evil spell that you will never break, boy, do you hear me?" The words fell upon a physically shaken, now mute and limp bully.

That's great, Mum, I think you have now guaranteed Cymon and me both the privilege of wearing dog feces daily for the rest of our natural lives. Thank you for your adult words of wisdom and motherly logic. May the ground please open up and take me down in a puff of red smoke with her when this mad old witch disappears.

The strange thing was, however, that due to the imaginations we all possessed, there was not one person witnessing this manic outburst that didn't believe her. Myself included. She was a frightening lady for sure, but a witch? She had now made that claim herself. Maybe it was her crooked nose and the terrifying level of her voice—maybe it was complete stupidity and overwhelming embarrassment in everyone involved—that did the trick. Whatever it was, the incident was never mentioned again. Ever. The feces stopped flying that very instant. It just became one of those playground legends that are whispered of occasionally but that nobody dares to recall at any kind of discernible volume around anyone remotely involved.

Was I really the son of Margaret Hamilton, Wicked Witch of the West, sometimes moonlighting as Wicked Witch of South London?

To this day I'm still not absolutely sure.

CHAPTER SIX

❧

INDIANA JONES AND THE TEMPLE OF DOOM, 1984

Directed by Steven Spielberg.
Prequel to Raiders of the Lost Ark, which follows the adventures of
1930's archaeologist Indiana Jones (Harrison Ford). In this film, the
renowned adventurer and expert in the occult teams up with a nightclub
singer and a twelve-year-old named Short Round. The story takes them
to an Indian village, where the people believe evil spirits have taken their
children away after a sacred stone has been stolen. A fun-filled
adventure ride albeit it a very dark subject matter. Academy Award
winner for Best Visual Effects.

Outings to the cinema gradually evolved into their own little routines. One such routine, which took place with my brother beside me in the car, was very annoying to our parents. While we traveled, and sat as still as we could (following our guardians' instructions to the tee), we did our best to find inventive ways to upset one another.

I would normally whistle. I was a true master of whistling. Magnificent blows. Never-ending-drawn-out-shrill. My whistling had very little to do with replicating a tune: mostly, it was a single note that I drew out tirelessly just to get to my brother, touching his delicate nerves in a very delicate place. When the whistling lost its effectiveness, the tone would seamlessly morph into hot air. I would press my face as close to Cymon's as I could and proceed to exhale as heavily as possible, as if I were sighing with the weight of the world. This fluid movement had to be perfectly choreographed, before he jolted me violently away. Just hearing the ludicrousness of his complaint to my mother that I "was breathing" on him was a pure source of entertainment for me, and one I gleefully repeated over and over at the slightest of opportunities.

Due to our tedious bickering my parents soon reached the end of the road, abruptly putting a stop to our beloved family outings. Unbeknownst to me, I would sadly be an adult before I ever set foot inside a cinema with my parents again. Public transportation, therefore, became the next—and really only—option for my brother and me, elevating us to young men now on their own cinematic journey.

The big day had finally come—could it be true, after waiting so many years? I was at last old enough, or at least by default allowed to go unaccompanied to the hallowed inner-sanctum of the cinema. Well, almost unaccompanied; I had my best friend Graham Tonkin in tow. As best friends go, he was the very best there was, hands down. He was a year older, and I thought at least one hundred years wiser, and had the added bonus of living only three doors away from me. With such close proximity to each other, we developed a secret signal to let each other know where we were at all times. Screw the phone system, we just didn't need it. Our signal was an odd sort of high-pitched, cockerel crowing noise that abruptly became obsolete when puberty came knocking. Then it evolved into more of a battered-foghorn-on-its-last-legs kind of sound. But it was still our own secret sign, something unique to us. The sweet sound of a desperate cockerel being strangled would come, seemingly from the heavens; an invite for me to come over and participate in some tomfoolery (as, of course, I always gladly did).

Graham grew up a good Irish-Catholic boy in a house of four older sisters, he being the only son. He attended my rival school, All-Saints, which was positioned at the top of a hill, on a road both of our schools shared. You can be sure that All-

Saints had very few little saints on its premises, let alone ALL of them. Maybe the naming convention was just a wishful projection by the local South London education authority.

Graham's house was the most bizarrely decorated homestead I have ever come across still to this day, but it all seemed very normal to me back then, and not one piece of the décor was ever questioned or laughed at. Lavish home accoutrements included thick, red velvet floral wallpaper, which gave a confining, wall-to-ceiling carpet feel throughout the house. A chandelier in the front room was fashioned into the shape of four illuminated ice cream cones (on a dimmer so you could set the ice cream to *mood lighting*). Scattered throughout was a variety of mass-produced oil paintings of exotic, half-naked women. Each of the pieces of art on display looked as though it were painted by cack-handed monkeys that had been blindfolded. Some of these paintings themselves were made of cheap velvet and thus were a perfect, quite uncanny match to the overwhelming wallpaper on which they hung. To top it all off, huge brass plates were randomly displayed throughout the house with *Ye-Olde-Yorkshire-Puddingy* English scenes hammered unskillfully onto their surfaces. It was the kind of useless kitchenware normally displayed only in dodgy country pubs that served no real purpose other than to bring the establishment's décor to a lower standard.

Graham's father, Michael Tonkin, was a builder by trade, so the house was always in a state of progress, with various bricks and a small sand pile littering the back garden. Mick's skin was weathered from labor and being in the sun all day: leathery, with a tan stain, and creviced well beyond his years. The tattoos of his youth now bled into a green, indistinguishable mass on his muscular arms. He was a man to be feared and

40

avoided once he drank his nightly brews, which clung stale to his breath throughout the day until they were refreshed the following evening. Nothing in the house was ever quite complete and, strangely, never finished throughout the ten years I spent in their homely palace.

Every school summer holiday, though, Graham and I would without fail have our annual falling out. You could almost set your watch by it. Playful words that had rolled off my back for the entire year would suddenly become hurtful and meaningful. Words in turn would become pushes, then more powerful shoves, developing into full-blown scuffling affairs. During these skirmishes, Graham bore a huge cheshire cat smile fixedly upon his face, one he had been saving up all year, to show how little of his strength he was using in my guaranteed defeat. Of course, I pretended not to care, but despite how hard I tried, my face would become immersed in a frown, and my chin gradually immersed into my chest, releasing a torrent of tears. This marked the end of the friendship, for a few days at least, until the pleasures of our famous cockerel call would reunite us in memories of past joys.

Strangely, for our first excursion alone to the cinema, we were making the treacherous journey to see fellow adventurer Indiana Jones and to find out what the hell the so-described *Temple of Doom* was all about. One could only fearfully imagine! With my parents finally now broken and no longer witnesses to my annoying breathing-humming self, Graham and I traveled on the red double-decker number 68 bus into Croydon.

My older brother (obviously sent on a reconnaissance mission by my parents to track me and Graham), plainly refused to be seen within a hundred yards of our presence. We both knew Cymon really had no interest in seeing this film, a fact he had not tried to conceal. He traveled begrudgingly to the cinema as instructed, with my parents watching us both step onto the bus that conveniently stopped in front of our house. A few stops down, though, my brother made his escape and switched to the bus traveling directly behind the one we were meant to be on. If he were really following our parents' instructions he would have needed to have some sort of Superman X-ray vision in order to not take his eyes off me. I thought this was a little strange at the time, but maybe he did have undisclosed abilities. He was, after all, a strange lad. Logic and a ten-year-old don't always walk the same narrow path. Maybe that cunning fox was himself trying to get some attention from the blonde ticket seller, taking a faster route to the cinema? Could my brother be capable of such utter family dishonesty and betrayal? Yes, most definitely.

The hype surrounding *Indiana Jones* had been building for months. One of my Indian (dots, not feathers) friends, Justin Patel, had actually been an extra in some scenes, and he proudly brought to school Harrison Ford's and Steven Spielberg's autographs to gloat about on the school playground. Pieces of actual paper they had touched, could it be true? As movie stars and directors go, there was no greater pairing, and Justin Patel, with his newly discovered popularity, knew this full well and, naturally, milked it for everything it was worth.

For months…

And months…

And months.

For a brief time, he had even ousted Thomas Burns, much to everyone's shock, and momentarily became the newly appointed playground storyteller. Justin relayed to us fantastical tales about the production of the film. He told us about his father eating chilled monkey brains, feasting on a starter of slippery semiconscious serpents, with boiled bug broth to wash it all down. Justin spoke of the occasional child being sacrificed on the set while filming, and naturally we didn't doubt him for a minute. Why should we? He was practically best friends with Han Solo, accomplice to Chewbacca the Wookie. If Harrison Ford felt trustworthy enough to present Justin with a signed piece of paper, the least I could do would be to trust the dodgy tales he was now hourly concocting.

On the day of the film's premiere in our little world, excitement had gotten the better of Graham and me, so much so that we arrived at the cinema hours before the movie even contemplated starting. The doors were firmly locked shut, but the exterior of the cinema proudly displayed movie posters to study, in which we would discover plot details from the carefully woven imagery. There was also a posted selection of stills from the movie, showing us the most pucker scenes, or, in other words, spoiling the best moments and special effects so we weren't too surprised or terrified by the movie magic. As an added bonus, on this occasion the movie gods were smiling down upon us with another good movie poster. Before us hung a magnificent "coming attraction" poster for the re-release of *Mary Poppins*, so of course we both tried our best to memorize the word *supercalifragilisticexpialidocious*, which was spelled across the entire length of the poster in colorful, dancing, happy Disney letters. However, after about five letters my mind suddenly became daunted with the task and blanked completely. I knew I could definitely spell the word *super* and determined that the rest of the word wasn't really any kind of useful everyday vocabulary, so what the hell did it matter anyway.

Career plans and life-altering directions throughout my childhood years were consistently dictated by the cinema and my favorite film at the time. I went from praying that I grew up to be a mouse after the highly emotional and utterly disturbing animated Disney film *The Rescuers*, to being sure my destiny was now in the field of archaeology after seeing *Indiana Jones and the Temple of Doom*. For a Spielberg movie, this one was a little bizarre, to say the least. Good old Spielberg, friend to children and families across the world, suddenly gave us images of children being whipped and imprisoned (just as Justin had described), being sacrificed and taken forcefully from their weeping relatives. Thanks a lot, Steven. If it's not the Wicked Witch scaring me to death, it's now you that can't be trusted! There goes my sleep pattern for another week. Leaving the cinema as a child I would be highly affected by what I had just seen, and with Spielberg being the master puppeteer of your every emotion, you could safely multiply your frenzied state by a hundred when viewing one of his offerings. With *Indiana Jones and the Temple of Doom* the effect on me would last for an entire, quite inspired week.

After witnessing the film, my archeological Indy phase consisted of digging what I thought was a massive hole in our back garden, in search for God knows what, but on the lookout nonetheless. For the first few days of my tiring expedition, I dug for hours, stopping only to watch *Wacky Races* and *Blue Peter* on television. Even an archeologist must have his priorities. My mum, on the other hand, wasn't at all amused at the sudden destruction of her garden and at the muddy footprints traipsed through her house toward the television set. I couldn't expect her to understand; how could she? Obviously, she was no trained archeologist. She had not borne witness to the terrific

44

Indiana Jones saga; after all, it was her choice to send me out alone to the cinema.

Somewhere between Wednesday and Thursday of that week after discovering nothing but mud and a couple of odd-shaped pebbles, my plans suddenly took a completely new direction. Enter my cunning childhood logic again. What the hell—if I kept digging I could reach Australia, or possibly even China (if I dug at a funny angle), and my family would all benefit from my tunnel. We could go on holiday for a few weeks, whenever we so desired. It would just mean driving the car into the muddy hole and exiting...wherever we wanted. Now my mum would surely understand my hours of hard toil and labor. I was still searching above all for a proud acknowledgment from her as she stared at the caked mud strewn in a path behind me.

I'm glad at this juncture in my life I'd never seen the film *Journey to the Center of the Earth*, as this might have thrown a large proverbial spanner in the works. Dinosaurs, lava, and scantily clad cave women all hiding out underneath us. Who knew? The arduous dig continued, backbreaking labor—night after endless night. And then I discovered it in all its glory, the thing I had been searching for all along. I uncovered...Friday, otherwise known as the beginning of the weekend! Totally dirty and completely knackered, all plans had been scrapped and I made the executive decision that my dig would remain—just a hole. A four-foot-deep hole for future generations to admire and gather around in awe at the sheer technical feat. A new South London landmark.

Still to this day a totally magnificent idea on paper. A holiday tunnel, a cheap excursion for families. How could you possibly argue? Ask the creators of the Channel Tunnel (who, of course, ruthlessly stole my idea and allowed thousands of families to enter a muddy hole outside London and end up in dirty France). You will be hearing from my lawyers, Chunnel-dream-stealers! Time would slowly hide my labors until they were again just a garden and a cinematic memory, reclaiming the land I had toiled over with apparent ease and slyness.

The nation had lost a great holiday hole, but there were more films, and more ideas sure to be garnered from the next cinematic offering to creep into my impressionable psyche. The only question that remained was which life direction would the next film thrust me into? With an excited fever and mud still under my nails, I waited for my new destiny to make itself apparent. I reveled in the riches of the newfound freedom in going to the cinema alone, quite unaware that I had actually paid the ultimate price. I had lost the experience of sharing the cinema with my family, a thing I had taken for granted. An innocent experience that later on in life I would have paid all the money in the world to buy back.

CHAPTER SEVEN

❧

E.T., 1982

Directed by Steven Spielberg.
A group of alien botanists visits Earth and E.T. (the extra-terrestrial)
gets lost and left behind. E.T. is soon found by a ten-year-old boy, Elliot
(Henry Thomas). The two find a universal way to communicate, and a
bond is formed. The alien learns about life on Earth and Elliot learns
about love and understanding. E.T., with the help of his new friends,
finds his way home. Academy Award winner for Best Visual Effects.

When we were not preoccupied with the important work of digging holes in the back garden, Graham and I used to spend many a night dicking around in the park. Grange Park to be precise. It was here that we would spend countless hours perched on our BMX bikes, conveniently just a short peddle from our houses. There was nothing really distinctive about my part of South London, and nothing distinguished our park from any one of the small grass-and-shrub patches that littered the area. The Thornton Heath suburb of Croydon was that sort of nondescript place, and Grange Park was that sort of dirty, glue-sniffing grassland.

After witnessing *E.T.*, a BMX bike was all every child in the neighborhood wanted. Steven Spielberg had swiftly created an outright frenzy among my friends, each of us clamoring for his own small piece of Americana. Paul Thompson was the neighborhood's oracle on all matters concerning BMXes. His vernacular included half-pipes, bunny-hops, pegs, skyway wheels, and other strange concoctions. Paul had perfected more tricks upon his bike than any tricky person deserved to fully master. Under his watch we all adorned our bikes with stickers and personalized touches, fastening crates to the handlebars so that they would mimic the bikes in the film. Each of us had a place specifically designed to carry his own alien, just in the event that one were to mysteriously fall into Thornton Heath. Between my friends and me, the little fella would not have to walk too far.

My red and white BMX beauty was proudly purchased from the local Raleigh bike shop, its proprietor being an aged Mr. Crag, with his thin, wispy, tobacco-stained hair. His small shop held the overwhelming scent of fresh rubber as you entered it, with people huddled among the bikes, waiting patiently to be served. It's not that business was booming; quite the contrary, in fact. Mr. Crag would appear from the back room dressed like a butcher, outfitted in a newly pressed white apron, looking confused and wide-eyed but always eager to help.

"Yes sir, can I help you?" he would ask with as much enthusiasm as he could muster.

The only problem with his question was that he was already helping you but had forgotten entirely what your request was. Moreover, he had completely forgotten who you were by the time he returned from the back room and retraced his steps to the counter.

"Yes sir, can I help you?"

"You're already helping me, Mr. Crag."

"Ah yes, what was it again?"

This would be the endless, frustrating dialogue that sent Mr. Crag scuttling once more into the back room, the sound of his enthusiastic footsteps diminishing as once again he forgot his purpose. And so the perpetual cycle went, day after day, with customers' patience wearing thin as they one by one drifted from his shop. You were indeed quite lucky to actually find Mr. Crag lucid enough so that you could purchase something from him. Making the occasional successful purchase from Mr. Crag only added another layer of novelty to my BMX bike, a tale to be shared among friends while balanced proudly on top of it.

Grange Park, unlike the sprawling, beautifully manicured park in *E.T.*, was positioned next to the standard lineup of local crap shops. Unfailingly, in every town, such shops consisted of:

1. A Pakistani-run newsagent, also known by the not-so-politically-correct term Paki-Shop.

2. An off-license.

3. A launderette.

And, of course…

4. A hairdresser.

With the occasional variant, these quintessential shops would be joined by a petrol station or, in our case, a bike shop. This extra amenity added a certain flair to the lucky neighborhood. We were one of the lucky ones, and the neighborhood shared a common pride for our local bonus establishment.

The Paki-Shop contained a huge assortment of Cadbury's chocolate delights that had become grossly affected in taste by the constant scent of curry in the air. The stench was always quite overwhelming as you entered the store, and the sweet chocolate tasted more of coriander than Cadbury's. To make some extra money I helped deliver the local papers (*The South London Press* and *The Croydon Advertiser*) for the Paki-Shop. More accurately, I was delivering for its proprietor, Mr. Gupta, thus taking on a laborious paper route. It was my first real job.

Gupta beamed his huge white smile every day, obviously oblivious to the remnants of curry that seemed always to be clinging to his cardigan. It was as if his clothes had been washed in paneer rather than Persil the previous night. In American films, the kids wheeled down the sun-soaked streets, tossing papers carelessly onto people's front yards. In England, though, it's a slightly more tedious task. If you threw anything into people's gardens, you were more likely to be punched than thanked for a delivery. Each paper had to be folded three times by hand, under the precise watch of Mr. Gupta in his shop, and then walked to each person's front door...usually in the pissing-down, freezing rain. In addition, there was the constant task of precariously avoiding attack dogs, no easy feat in itself.

My fluorescent orange delivery bag would be loaded so heavily that it would quite literally slice into my shoulder as I wobbled down the street on my bike. I was convinced that Gupta did this to make sure that he got his absolute money's worth every day. I soon discovered that dumping the papers in a rubbish bin was a lot less work and much easier on my body, so I began, unbeknownst to the Paki-Shop, to earn a living folding and then discarding the local happenings instead of bringing forth the local news. Grange Park, and not the workplace, after all, was the best place to make use of my new pride and joy—my gleaming BMX bike.

In addition to the park, the Paki-Shop, and the off-license (where you could go without your parents and buy single cigarettes as long as you were old enough to at least walk on your own), there was the launderette. It provided us with another great hangout establishment if the park suddenly lost its interest. The launderette was where we traded secret factoids about women (or tarty girls, anyway) and challenged each other with tests of human strength...usually resulting in a competition of how many pull-ups we could do on the clothes-hanging bars. On average, two pull-ups was my best. Well, about one and a half, really. Pretty pathetic. The only person I was impressing was the owner of this fine establishment, with the fact that I *wasn't* breaking his pull-up-bar-general-laundry utility. Most importantly, however, the launderette allowed Graham and I to watch beautiful women actually handling their very own bras and knickers as they put them into the wash. Pure adolescent heaven.

Lastly, there was the local hairdresser. The shop's name was poorly fastened over the previous establishment's signage, both intermingling when illuminated at night. The current hairdresser's sign was emblazoned with the wonderfully catchy name *Hair Today, Gone Tomorrow*. I will never understand the business's survival to this day. The previous salon had lasted less than a year, and it seemed as though this new shop was resting its financial dreams purely upon a ridiculous name, obviously stumbled upon while drunk. I never witnessed one person enter or leave the shop throughout my years of living in the neighborhood.

There were no major landmarks that could help you pinpoint your location in the not-so-majestic surrounding area of Thornton Heath. There was, however, the clock tower. It was the closest thing we had to a landmark, this tower. Home to…a clock. Like a tiny *Big Ben*, maybe *Little Ben*, or even more appropriately, *Boring Ben*. Even so, it was not very exciting as a main focal point in the town, but it was nonetheless meaningful to us lads because it marked the entrance to Grange Park, a time and place for pure fun.

Having at this point reached that age where I felt most at home perched on my bike, I would only occasionally allow myself to be observed in the Grange Park playground. These once-magical forms of entertainment were now far in my juvenile past. I could only now justify playing on the kid's stuff in the park under certain stringent conditions. These would combine:

1. A dalliance with death.

2. A dare or double-dare issued by an accomplice involving the possibility of a severe head trauma on the tarmac.

3. The very real prospect of impressing a girl I couldn't imagine actually speaking to.

So, I rose to the challenge by riding the children's entertainment at near g-force speeds…occasionally. Most impressive, however, was the fact that during these death-defying stunts I was balancing a Benson and Hedges fag from my mouth (bought singularly, of course), my eyes scanning my friends' sisters for any kind of acknowledgment. The prospect of causing major grievous bodily harm to yourself seemed to defeat the playground's childish reality, a feat worth putting my BMX bike down for. It became something that wasn't completely beneath me even at eleven, nearly a FULLY GROWN man.

Along with the onslaught of bikes, the park also seemed to be letting in more of the female species through its rusty gates. A daily testosterone procession of girls, each walking hand in hand with a new female accomplice. But that wasn't the only place they were showing up; they were flipping all over! There was also a sudden change when it came to the films that Graham and I wanted to watch. Films had suddenly developed breasts, legs, and beautiful, round, squidgy bottoms. One minute the dwarfs in

Snow White were so funny and cute, each distinct with lovable Disney traits, and the next minute we were fascinated with Snow White's bodice and its contents. It was almost as if one moment films didn't contain girls, and the next moment you just couldn't miss them in all their voluptuous glory. It seemed as though instantly films had become *very* different; there was definitely something unsettling hanging in the South London air.

But what exactly had changed? Why all of a sudden was I taking more interest in the selection of my bike-riding attire? Was my hair looking good? Would the white toweling top, adorned with a pattern of blue polar bears, suddenly become appealing to the opposite sex? To be frank, I couldn't see why not. It was the closest thing to a BMX uniform that I could lay my hands on in London, mimicking Elliot's clothing from the film *E.T.* as meticulously as possible. My mother soon began to detest the polar bear top, as I wouldn't take it off for weeks, rescuing it constantly from the ruthless laundry basket until it was ready to be fumigated rather than laundered. She repeatedly reached the point where she would prohibit me from wearing it, which meant to me, of course, that I wore it everywhere she couldn't see me.

Another sudden change was my development of a very wobbly voice, which arrived quite unannounced like an annoying relative. I knew it was somehow related to me, I just couldn't for the life of me think how. My warbling voice meant I now spoke as little as possible, answering questions with the wink of an eye or a nod of the head or, more impressively and quite randomly, popping a wheelie to show off for the girls. I also had developed a growing awareness of my lower region, which I knew could also be blamed on the park tarts. It seemed as though my willie had itself become hostage to their cunning plan. Did these park tarts know no sanctity?

Quite clearly women were infiltrating my simple life, not just breaking down the gates of Grange Park. Words uttered by this beautiful amazon race suddenly all had sexual connotations, and to accompany them, a whole new set of tight, revealing clothing everywhere I looked. It felt as though thousands of years of evolution had rapidly progressed, leaving me behind in the park clinging onto my BMX tightly. The whole cinematic experience was just different now. I found myself paying as much attention to the girls surrounding me in the cinema as I did the actual film. I now actually went to the cinema to study all I could about this strange breed.

I was soon taught the art of kissing a girl via the medium of film. It seemed best to begin the process with a heavy argument and a short tussle. Quite randomly, all movement would stop so you could stare at each other for a few seconds. Next, there would be a subtle sign—the head leaning. This was usually followed by the slow move-in and then, suddenly, plenty of tongue and roughness. Graham eloquently described this kind of kiss as "slap and tickle." It would throughout the years take on further ridiculous name incarnations, but the game remained much the same.

I was aware that I was like a sponge absorbing all knowledge as fact thrown at me from films: my sexual tutors had previously been Dorothy and the Scarecrow, Baloo and Mowgli, Princess Leia and Han Solo, and now, of course, most recently Elliot and E.T. Were there really better people on this planet to learn kissing from? Some of the girls I found myself surrounded with and uncomfortable around even resembled E.T., but the ultimate question still remained: How on earth would I get this newly discovered alien breed to notice me?

Grab the BMX and pop a wheelie...works every time.

CHAPTER EIGHT

❧

THE ELEPHANT MAN, 1980

Directed by David Lynch.
Based on the true story of John Merrick (John Hurt) about a nineteenth-century Englishman afflicted with a disfiguring disease that transformed his features into something monstrous. The kindly Dr. Frederick Treves (Anthony Hopkins) rescues Merrick and begins to introduce him to society, and the audience watches as he attempts to regain the dignity he lost after years spent as a sideshow freak.

My time at Cypress Junior School inevitably came to an end due to the natural progression of school hierarchy. I was about to leave behind the tiny classrooms and the girls, who had just become apparent to me not only in Grange Park but also peeking out from behind their schoolbooks. I was already feeling nostalgic for junior school life at the mere thought of senior school, knowing that adult responsibility would inevitably be chasing me close behind. I had, after all, now borne witness to films like *Kramer vs. Kramer*, *The Graduate*, *Nightmare on Elm Street*, and *Teen Wolf*, all of which taught me that adulthood would be no simple ride!

Every morning at junior school I had become accustomed to enduring a full school assembly. This consisted of hundreds of kids forced to sit crossed-legged with their arms folded in their laps, pretending to listen attentively to the dribble that poured from the headmistress's mouth. Her name was Mrs. Dakin—an all-too benign and unassuming name for our stern school matriarch. She was a harsh woman in every sense of the word. Harshness seeped from her every action, every breath, even from her physical features. The trait was especially noticeable when she chose to ridicule you at close range in front of the entire assembly. Each child's face crumpled the same way, doing its best to fold in on itself, fruitlessly trying to avoid the inevitable showering of saliva and stench that came from the depths of the disciplinarian's rotting body.

Assemblies led by Mrs. Dakin would, in her mind, be overflowing with poignant information, but in reality they were merely stupid anecdotes on bustling junior school life, and a recipe of pure tedium dished up from 9:15 to 9:45 a.m. daily. It was here that we sang ludicrous Christian songs, including the classics: "The Ink Is Black—The Page Is White," "Cross Over the Road My Friend—Ask the Lord His Thanks to Lend," and my favorite, "Little Donkey Carry Mary." Ah, yes— this delicious ass-laden song was a little Christmas treat to which we would heavily inflect every other word, for reasons which surely were as simple as being able to shout and not be reprimanded. It was the kind of overemphasis usually reserved for the line FIVE GOLDEN RINGS! in the classic *The Twelve Days of Christmas*.

To help break the seemingly endless monotony of morning assembly you would pray that there would be *some* injection of spontaneity. Just one well-timed trumpet of flatulence, or at least the screaming of highland obscenities at random, courtesy of Mrs. Johnson (Mrs. Dakin's partner in crime, an utterly insane and uncontrollable old Scottish woman.) She would endow us with her screams on the not-so-rare occasions when she would catch someone falling asleep in a key moment in one of Mrs. Dakin's speeches, startling the guilty party and thus pulling him or her from the hall by a clump of their hair or an ear. Thankfully, this happened on a regular basis, interrupting the Christian sermons. But then again, nothing was sacred at Cypress Junior School. Yes, indeed, we were the pride of South London.

During an assembly in my final year, Mrs. Dakin proudly announced the news of "a very-very generous donation" that had been bestowed upon the school. Cypress Junior had been given the original brass school bell, now proudly once more back under school lock and key. It was a huge, ornate piece newly finished and restored to its original glory from over two hundred years ago.

"God was smiling upon our school once more," Mrs. Dakin orated, her voice cracking as she spoke with the religious passion she adored. "And we will show our appreciation by ringing our thanks back to the heavens."

While struggling to control her tears, Mrs. Dakin informed us that one deserving student each morning would have the chance to ring the bell, calling the assembly and children to order. In her mind this task was the ultimate reward for good work and, most importantly, a model for good Christian behavior. And so it was to be. The bell was hung proudly with its accompanying red, white, and blue bellpull outside her office and rung generously each morning for about...two days. At that point, the school was mysteriously broken into and the bell vanished. God apparently had realized his mistake and was smiling down upon us no longer. It eventually reappeared six months later in an unlikely and inconspicuous place—it was displayed for sale in my friend's father's antique shop, who had a sudden lapse in memory as to how he obtained it. From that point on, Mrs. Dakin refrained from disseminating any details in regards to removable, valuable objects for fear that the information would eventually make its way back to the parents.

The only time assemblies were even remotely fun was once a month when Mrs. Dakin would relinquish her duties and allow a class to perform for the rest of the school. It was here

57

that I first witnessed a member of my own family on stage. My brother Cymon was performing a literary classic. Lo and behold, Cypress Junior School's presentation of...*Star Trek.*

Cymon's class's production was an adaptation of the television series, complete with tight-fitting sixties costumes and a cardboard Starship Enterprise spaceship. The tiny actors threw themselves violently from side to side on stage, magically creating the illusion that a spaceship was crashing onto an alien planet. The ridiculous debacle that ensued was quite a treat for those of us tired of Mrs. Dakin's verbal diarrhea.

My brother (not only a dysfunctional child but also playing the part of a dysfunctional robot) made his grand entrance,plodding onto the stage with a mission: to take control of Mr. Spock (who himself appeared complete with cardboard pointy Vulcan ears). Cymon's custom-made costume consisted of a painted Safeway washing powder box which he wore on his head and from which protruded a vast array of copper cables. He walked like an out-of-control breakdancer ripped from the film *Breakdance 2: Electric Boogaloo.* There had, however, been one small point overlooked by the ingenious *Blue Peter* double-sided-sticky-tape costume designer. The eyeholes weren't cut out properly in his intergalactic helmet, and consequently my brother couldn't see the edge of the stage, even with his robot vision. The future, quite literally, was obviously not too bright for his particular species of androids. Cymon made his grand entrance and continued walking right off the edge of the stage, landing in a pile of twisted cardboard and copper cables directly by my feet and to the delighted laughter of hundreds of children. It really was quite hard to decipher who was more humiliated between the two of us. *Beam me up, Scotty.*

The school performances were not all bad, though. The ones that involved girls were a whole different story. It was during one such performance that I witnessed my first love, a girl whose name to this day I am still unsure of. She will always remain to me a nameless heavenly creature, out of reach and forever behind the velvet curtain. I had spotted her a few times at the park where she was a vision among the trees—smoking fags and spitting out excess saliva with perfect aim. Now she had pride of place in the school's tropical performance, dressed in a costume of yellow bird feathers and perched upon a cardboard branch. She was a beauty with golden feathers fluttering in the breeze, and she sang "Yellow Bird" to an assembly full of adoring fans—how could I have *not* fallen for her?

She was older and obviously wiser than me, and from that moment on, whenever I saw her at the park or within the narrow hallways at school, I suddenly forgot how to perform basic human motor skills. I hardly knew the girl. Actually, that is a little misleading. I didn't know her at all, and I soon realized she would never stoop to my level and take an interest in me. I had more of a chance of ringing the old school bell than I ever did of speaking to her! She would always be out of my reach and up on a pedestal (err…branch?), and, quite honestly, I just didn't know how to behave around this…bird.

Not having a BMX wheelie to bail me out of the situation, there were a number of other schoolboy options to choose from. I chose to adopt the most common technique: It was the Shy-Boy Maneuver. This consisted of tucking my chin deep into my chest whenever our paths crossed so as not to actually ever make eye contact with her disapproving glare. I had also developed an extreme case of eczema at this very delicate age, which added to my insecurities. The fact that I itched and scratched uncontrollably when I was even slightly flustered added to my ridiculousness. My skin would flare up in red, sore patches, and it was constantly cracking, bleeding, and flaking from my body. The skin which I inhabited quite literally became too small for me. The condition crumbled not only my skin but also my confidence, so, naturally, the last thing I wanted was to have the yellow bird actually notice my interest in her or, more disturbingly, notice my mutating body. I was now hiding from myself as much as I was hiding from her beautiful presence.

And then it happened—she spoke, vocalizing the only tender words of love she would ever utter to me as our arms briefly touched in the hallway.

"Look where you're going, you double-chinned leper!" she barked with annoyed conviction as our star-crossed lovers' paths collided.

It's amazing the effect a person so young can have on another human being. If only I knew her name, I swear to God, I would have tracked her down and sent her the bill for the plastic surgery I would get later in life to rectify my chin and skin conditions.

Feathery Bitch.

I was completely devastated. It seemed as though my life had taken the darkest of turns. All that was seemingly important to me was also completely repulsed by me and thus intangible. Was I really the epitome of grotesque? Images flashed through my mind which placed me among my brethren: *Frankenstein*, *The Phantom of the Opera*, *The Hunchback of Notre Dame*, and *The Elephant Man*. Was I to be cast aside and shunned for the rest of my days alongside such film horrors, living my life under an X-rated certificate?

As an adult, I can barely remember a thing about the girl from which such cruelty came. Was her skin really as yellow as her given name would suggest? It's probably healthier that I've replaced my memory of her with that of Snow White's witch and a strange amalgamation of girls I would fall for along the winding path of life, each bird in someway sculpting me into a man. Relationships for me now are less verbally callous; sometimes my skin is less repulsive… or at least thicker anyway. Come to think of it, traces of that yellow bird can be found in every romance that has flown into my life to this day. I do still find myself panicked and looking for yellow feathers somehow hidden from sight when a relationship becomes serious… but only every now and again.

On a brighter note, since that devastating moment of collision, I have never again had to traipse uncomfortably toward a girl in a school hallway, moving as if I was somehow trapped in *The Elephant Man* body. Well—not exactly.

My focus had been diverted from film, something that was never cruel to me, and replaced by females, or more precisely a girl that chose to be nothing but cruel. Bollocks. I realized that I needed to find pleasant girls. I needed to watch kind films. I needed to think logically of a solution.

Jimmy Saville. Write to the television show *Jim'll Fix It*— he would surely have the answer to my conundrum.

CHAPTER NINE

🕮

GHOSTBUSTERS, 1984

Directed by Ivan Reitman.
After being kicked out of their university, parapsychology professors
Spengler (Harold Ramis), Stantz (Dan Aykroyd), and Venkman
(Bill Murray) decide to go into business together trapping and removing
ghosts from New York City's haunted buildings. The three soon find their
business booming and take on more work than they can handle.
Ghostbusters becomes the first multimillion-dollar scare comedy.

Ghostbusters was the first film I actually attended with someone of the opposite sex. It was also the first film in which I really had no interest. Blasphemy! The playground at Sylvan Senior School was rife with preposterous stories of how girls behaved in dark cinemas with my swaggering friends. Girls supposedly even collaborating in the cinema with the loosening of their skirts and the sucking in of their stomachs, providing easier access to their top-secret girly bits.

I had heard that the back row of the cinema was the place to be; a line countless boys had crossed where girls became willing participants to young testosterone fantasies and heavy-handed explorations. The problem with these revelations for me was that I found myself completely sexually uninitiated up until this point; they were just—stories. Now, logically, I didn't want to be left completely at the starting line. I wanted to experience the significance of a snog for myself in a dark cinema, so I set about the task of finding a suitable guinea pig. Just not too much of a pig. Obviously.

My unfortunate candidate was Sylvan School's very own Joanne Hardy. She was by all accounts a *pleasant* girl. Not a beauty, but definitely not a dog—just...*pleasant*. She had the obligatory sensible-girl shoes, carried a sensible pencil case, wore a sensible school uniform, and had other pleasant friends. It was all really very agreeable indeed. When a girl's most endearing factor is her pleasantness, you tend to seek out other, smaller things to help justify lusting after her. For Joanne Hardy that winning factor was the little Marilyn Monroe-1980's-Madonna mole she had, perfectly placed under her nose. That was all it took; the deal was signed, sealed, and soon would be delivered, if all went according to plan at the cinema that Saturday. I don't know why this facial inconsistency was so appealing to me, but it was all I needed. It could have been a dodgy ballpoint pen accident that caused it or it could have been a crusty, hanging bogey, but it was without a doubt the deal breaker. Saying that, though, this wasn't the only factor, to be fair to nice Miss Hardy—she had also developed breasts.

There was a definite time in school, very specifically as if another scheduled lesson, where girls all began to go through that special bodily change. Accompanying the metamorphosis came also a change in fashion and posture. Baggy clothes were hung upon their youthful frames in an effort to conceal the change in their chests, only enhancing our attention and curiosity. For us lads the fascination with breasts grew daily with the very breasts themselves. I was getting tired of hearing my friends question me as to whether I'd "gotten a leg over" or, of course, if I had "shagged a bird." Everyone was hungrily fishing for information, but no one had any to offer of his own. There were always the urban myth keepers on the playground spreading their nasty tales. Their beautiful romantic stories went something like this:

"Do you know what a rainbow kiss is? Because girls love it, they gag for it, and you have to give it to them." Rainbow kiss?

Let me think—a rainbow kiss? Nope. Must have missed that fascinating sexual explanation in biology.

"Well, a rainbow kiss is how they do it in Russia, where the man puts his tongue so far down the woman's throat that she vomits into his mouth in a rainbow of carrots and such, which, of course, he then has to drink to prove how much he loves her."

Straight from the lips of Michael Nolan, keeper of all sexual knowledge. Was he having a laugh? Michael with this nugget officially crossed the line of tall tales, at least that was what I hoped when he explained it to me. PLEASE tell me he was making this up...

"Really," I paused. "But I hate carrots!"

"You haven't done it yet?" he asked incredulously.

Michael would then persist, making fun of my inexperience. Naturally, I bragged that I had done everything, really.

This would always digress into the old staple response, "Well I've done it to your mother if that counts."

Then the obligatory mother-cussing would escalate for the rest of the break until the bell signaled the beginning of another type of lesson. I prayed harder than I've ever prayed before that Joanne Hardy wasn't a vegetarian, just to keep the rainbow colors to an absolute minimum. The following day during the lunch break I mustered up the courage to ask her out as she stood there with her regular gaggle of pleasant girlfriends. With my heart pounding, my cheeks flushed, and my mouth as dry as a Welshman's humor, I swooped in for the kill. I would have to woo her with my cunning linguistic skills. I was a true master of vocabulary, weaving together the very beautiful sounds of the English language, uttered as if they were stolen from a classic Shakespearian sonnet:

"Alright? Oi, do you want some Juicy Fruit chewing gum?"

And then there was that old, awkward classic: "I'm going to see…um…*Ghostbusters* this Saturday…er…do you want to come?" To which she was obviously swept off her feet, and thus surprisingly agreed to participate in my totally *un-nice* sexual exploits.

Like a military strategist I planned my attack on her body for days leading up to D-cup Day. Taking every possible scenario of the maneuver into account so I could tactically take the mounds on her chest that I knew would be inevitably heavily guarded.

The Odeon cinema in Croydon possessed an added bonus for many a father on a Saturday afternoon movie jaunt. A winning factor cunningly thought up by its corporate office's marketing genius, also an alcoholic. Presented on the entire landing of the second floor a vision awaited you, almost as if it was a mirage coming into view as you ascended the staircase right outside the heavy, swinging doors to cinema number two. A fully stocked, fully operational, fully licensed bar with the obligatory stale nuts laid out at specific intervals along its massive polished length. The sweet smell of stale alcohol seeped up from the red stained carpets, greeting your nostrils before you were allowed to enter the hallowed gates of theater two. The ticket ripper stationed at these doors always seemed a little jollier on this level, as if a main part of his job was to get completely wankered when all tickets had been ripped. This man obviously loved his job, at very regular intermissions.

When we entered the cinema that Saturday afternoon, Joanne and I were directed to the ascending staircase; we walked side-by-side closely, but not daring to actually touch in the harsh light of the foyer. Heaven forbid, I couldn't let on to Miss Nice that I actually liked her! She was going to think I was completely insane, going from a touching phobic to an out-of-control animal, wanting to touch everything and anything, just because the lights had gone down and we were in the back row. I just couldn't bring myself to reach out and take her delicate hand—I needed to calm myself quickly as my thoughts and sweaty palms were soon getting ahead of me. As we reached the top of the staircase our nostrils filled with the scent of liquor, but also a strange mess greeted our eyes. Beermats. A mutating collection of them strewn randomly across the carpet.

Absolutely everywhere.

I knelt down to further inspect them, only to find the pinnacle of film advertising genius. *Ghostbusters* beermats…who had thought that one up? This was a kid's film! It would be just as bad if Disney had *Bambi* Whiskey behind the bar…it just didn't seem to fit. But these were no ordinary beermats, they were cardboard mats—with a twist. The now-classic *Ghostbusters* logo had been transformed into a half-pissed ghost with a pint glass in his hand all packaged nicely together under the line "*Ghostbusters*, raise your spirits." Then it hit me. Quite literally.

There was such a mess on this hallowed ground because not only were these beermats amazingly mis-marketed, but much more importantly they could be thrown at a high velocity though the air like frisbees, striking people on the head and proving very useful in the end for mischievous kids. It just so happened that my head was in the way at this particular moment. What a great start to the groping. Now this nice girl must have thought I was a beermat cleptomaniac, with an aversion to touching, and lover of objects propelled directly toward my skull. Could this day really get any better? What was not to love about me? I needed to get inside the swinging doors quickly before the whole breast plan went completely flat.

"Where do you want to sit?" she asked me as our eyes adjusted to the light. Where do I want to sit? Was she taking the piss now? Surely we were on the same page. Of course, I tried to scope out the cinema, looking puzzled, pondering as if trying to garner where the best view would be for the cinematic main attraction.

"Um...how about right at the far back? In the corner?" I less than subtly suggested.

"Oh.....................okay," Joanne nicely, but decidedly tentatively, replied.

Come on, Nice Girl, at least try to act enthusiastic about this groping. We walked together, still not touching, as if in slow motion toward the dark depths of the cinema, to the much-whispered-about, infamous back row. My eyes caught the jealousy on every other boy's face that turned to stare at us as we trudged onward and upward. Finally, the moment of truth was nigh. But when to unleash the plan? Should I at least let her sit first?

We took our seats and tried to act as natural as possible, as if this was something we participated in every weekend. This was where the proverbial spanner was unleashed and thrown into the works. When we initially sat we were in the depths of the cinema, in the dark, all alone. Within seconds we were surrounded by a bunch of idiots, with handfuls of the ridiculous *Ghostbusters* beermats.

Why don't you pathetic imbeciles all FUCK OFF and leave us alone? Go back to watching your McDonald's Happy Meal of a kid's movie, or go play with your sodding beermats around some other retard that doesn't have a bloody bird to grope!

Of course, I didn't actually say this out loud, but you can be sure I was screaming it in my head. What I actually chose to do was just sit there and be completely silent, dumbfounded by how awry my well-thought-out plans were going. The lads taunted us constantly with sexual obscenities and made bold, swift attempts themselves to grab Joanne's chest. Oi! Wait in line, you idiots, this was my idea! I had entered into this with a carefully conceptualized, tactical plan, whereas these morons had arrived with the old staple—smash-and-grab. I had been totally blindsided by the idiot brigade. This was the one time I would have loved the cinema chair to just fold back and swallow me up, to provide a well-deserved escape route from the beermats they threw at my head at point-blank range. Strangely enough the escape route was ultimately provided by Joanne herself, punching one of the boys in the nose with a swift, hard, direct punch, creating a fountain of blood after a brave lunge forward by him that ended in tears. Bloody hell girl! That's not very nice now is it?

Needless to say, that afternoon my biology study was a complete disaster. I had failed the exam before I even got a chance to take it. The school's Miss Nice Joanne Hardy had turned about face, becoming Little Miss Nasty, uttering her beautiful farewell words, "You fucking wanker!" and never speaking to me again, disappearing off into the busy Croydon streets that sunny Saturday. I went to the cinema that day to get a well-deserved feel of Joanne's breasts, yet I left there feeling like a complete tit myself. Now I understood the relevance of the bar, and I could use a drink. I perched myself high on a bar stool and ordered a Coca-Cola, with no ice, which was swiftly delivered to me and placed upon a *Ghostbusters* beermat.

How annoying.

CHAPTER TEN

THE KARATE KID, 1984

Directed by John G. Avildsen.
The new teenager in town, Daniel (Ralph Macchio) is beset by bullies but determined to stick up for himself and get the girl. He begins to teach himself karate, only to discover that the caretaker in his building is a grand master in martial arts. Mr. Miyagi (Pat Morita) shows Daniel that there is more to karate than violence. This movie is another real crowd-pleaser from the director of the original Rocky.

As one can imagine, films such as *The Karate Kid* and *Rocky* wreaked havoc on the bodies of young moviegoers. With this type of action-extravaganza film, I walked into the cinema a mere mortal little man and left (or should I say ran) from the movie karate-kicking and punching my way to the local Croydon championship belts. It didn't matter how quiet or well-behaved a child you were upon entering the cinema for one of these films, it was guaranteed that all would leave physically abusing anyone or anything that happened to be within arm's reach.

A dark, foreboding time hung before me like an ominous cloud precariously balanced over my head, swelling and pulsating. I had now reached my milestone first teenage year in South London. Every part of my body was in a race with another, only to be aided by the testosterone-filled movies I viewed and reviewed. My innocent weekend jaunts to the cinema had become infested with Croydon's lowlifes calling me forward and sheltering me under their dirty little wings. And I loved every minute of it, of course. East Croydon possessed many shady characters, all centralized around a very dodgy street market. It was here that any imaginable stolen goods could be bought from shifty men with large, battered, brown suitcases at all hours of the day.

Every now and again a window of opportunity would open as the police turned their backs for a minute, and the street vendors hurriedly passed off their *borrowed* wares to the ever-eager public. Hoarse voices strained on every corner, "Oi, sweetheart…geezer come back will be the cry, when the man with the gifts passes you by!" echoing through the bedraggled streets. This totally and utterly fascinated me. Men that looked like they could barely afford a pair of shoes would have a case stashed full of alligator loafers and gold chains to match. A suitcase full of shiny Rolex watches could be seen being dished out by a man wearing a tatty plastic Casio timepiece with a smooth line to match: "Stolen love? No no no…do I look like the type of man that would steal anything? Maybe just your heart, darling. You're on a need-to-know basis love, and all you need to know is you're getting a fantastic deal."

And with the wink of an eye and the nod of a head you had yourself a bargain. Each vendor's voice was baritone, yet they were all very distinct from one another. The voices were gravelly from a day filled with bursts of loud, excitable dialogue and nervous chain-smoking. The cash passed quickly from hand to hand, each note added individually to the dirty crumpled pile, held firmly in place by a taut rubber band.

Both Graham's and my enthusiasm for the free shows the vendors put on for their adoring public didn't go unnoticed; far from it. We had quickly become a part of the act, an offshoot of the team with our youthful innocence being our best selling point. We both looked as though we had stepped out of the *Brady Bunch*, but in reality we were more at home with the Shady Bunch. What better use for two angelic kids—pretty much shielded from the law by our age—than to have them strategically placed upon each end of the street and used as lookouts for the annoying local law enforcement. Pure genius. And for this prestigious working-class job we were given a couple of quid and a pat on the back, and we got the chance to feel like hardened criminals, albeit for a few hours. Could life get any better? Hell, I would have paid *them* for this opportunity.

Graham and I also had our new whistling code down, replacing the prepubescent cockerel crow now long since discarded. Two sharp bursts were whistled out in the event of a possible "Copper!" sighting, and three longer spouts followed if it was a positive sighting of a "Rozza!" Our cinematic routine had officially changed. Instead of providing us with a feast of new movies to consume on Saturdays, the weekends provided us with a crop of stolen merchandise. Our job was to protect and allow for easy distribution of it to the punters. This new adventure had muscled its way into our lives cunningly and masterfully, leaving us quite unaware of its true long-term effects. We felt, of course, that all was going swimmingly well in our criminal world, until one fateful day when we inevitably got a little ahead of ourselves.

After a Saturday filled with hard graft (standing aimlessly on street corners with ever-suspicious eyes), we decided to step up our illegal activities a bit, whack 'em up the proverbial notch. Our criminal minds seemed to know no bounds, and then a stunningly bad idea dawned upon us, which we convinced ourselves was of a brilliant one. Instead of catching the red 68 bus back to our respective homes, we decided to go to the BMX shop down the street and steal something. Not out of any overwhelming need or desire, just because we could,

71

plain and simple. There you have it, an absolutely fantastic idea that needed to be realized.

We stealthily entered Halford's bike shop on Croydon's high street and proceeded to look for our loot. What excellent thing could I possibly need? Anything and everything was now ripe for the taking. A shop full of high-priced BMX bikes and accessories, too numerous to mention, was laid out on a platter before me. I studied everything as if I were a BMX scholar, my eyes flitting across the multitude of colors and shapes as if they were priceless faceted gems. Then in the flash of an eye it happened. In my peripheral vision I saw Graham's hand reach out and grab something and place it under his coat, and then he was out of the store walking down the street. Bloody hell, wait a minute mate! I'm not even close to being ready. Now for my glorious snatch. What better loot than…hmmm…a sheet of BMX stickers, priced at a massive one pound—or at a special discounted price of nothing for me.

Do it. *Quickly!*

My stealing reflex kicked in, and my arm gracefully reached out, missing the stickers and clanking into the metal shelf. However, on the swift return swing they were all mine. As if suddenly wearing horse blinders, I headed for the exit toward the front of the shop. Simple. A pro. A criminal mastermind in the making. The wind now blowing my hair in the street, and I was surrounded by the seemingly adoring masses. The only thing holding me back was an unexpected, aggressive tug on my collar. "I'm sorry. I'll pay for it, I'll pay for it!" were the only discernible words that next left my mouth while the spotty young manager of the store held on to me as if clutching the Holy Grail. Oh bugger. With his huge sausage fingers tightening around me, fear released my flood gates: tears streamed down my face and my throat swelled, suddenly making the act of breathing a chore. I was led back into the store and deposited in a locked room while the very authorities I had been watching out for were swooshing down to watch over me. Could I really be this much of a tit?

I sat there with a vivid image of my partner in crime at home, making new additions to his pristine BMX, while I sat waiting for the dirty coppers to arrive. You have to keep in mind, putting principle aside here, we are talking about a pathetic set of tiny, holographic BMX stickers, valuable only to the sticker manufacturer himself. I thought the bike shop was taking the piss, just playing with me, a harsh yet boisterous company scare tactic. Of course, I believed this right up until the point the police swung open the door to my makeshift cell. With a wry smile the policeman proceeded to handcuff me, called my mum (here we go), and then frog-marched me to the waiting Black-Mariah police van as if in slow motion, a condemned man. I knew that once my mother was involved I most certainly would be condemned. I was swiftly transported to a stinking police cell and given food under the door as if in a prison film, images of *Stir Crazy* and *The Great Escape* flashing through my mind. There I sat pondering my fate, trying to concoct an alibi, delicately scratching the paint off my jacket's buttons, my double chin sunk deeply into my chest.

It was here I sat.

And sat.

And sat.

The bell had been rung. Let the harsh punishment my mum was surely concocting commence.

My mother, in all of her wisdom, had decided she wouldn't pick me up at all. The police needed to release me to my legal

73

guardians, and so to add to the ridiculousness of the grand-BMX-one-pound-sticker theft, a classic Western standoff thus ensued. It felt like I was there for days, and quite honestly I may well have been. Negotiations continued through the night, my meals still slid through the door until my parents reluctantly arrived. My mother, when eventually I laid eyes on her, was acting strangely calm and controlled, speaking each word in almost a whisper, a smile anchored to her face like no smile I had seen before on a living thing. There was nothing happy or joyous about this smile, just a forced upturn in the side of her lips as if she were trapping something within the confines of her mouth.

We walked from the police station's sterile walls back into freedom. Nelson Mandela, now I understand your plight, my brother. There—that wasn't so bad.

Wwwwhhhhaaaaacccccckkkkk.

My mother unleashed her disappointment, now a screaming banshee beating me around the head with both fists clenched tightly, the whites of her knuckles radiant until I sobbed enough to satisfy her sadistic desires. She forbade me from ever talking to Graham Tonkin (best friend and slightly better thief than me) again. During the pauses in the beating I watched her mouth move, making sure I looked her attentively in the eye as if I were a naughty puppy, completely oblivious to the word forms that left her mouth.

My parents' solution in response to my out-of-control behavior was, as they eloquently put it, "A new outlet for my anger." What anger? What are you talking about? I just felt like nicking something; why is that so difficult for everyone to understand? And what was their ingenious idea, their solution to my problem? It was one which led me down a dimly lit path in London, to the doors of the local boxing club where I was easily half the age of the youngest meathead fighter there. *Rocky III* was still fresh in my mind from the cinema days before this tsunami of a crime wave, and now, as a hardened criminal, I thought I definitely possessed the eye of the tiger. So let the fighting begin—bring it on tough guys! Little did I know at this juncture that the only real tie I had to *Rocky* was a Mr. T phrase. I was a *fool* and definitely needed *pitying* after a few rounds in the ring.

The road to the *Rocky* championship belt was going to be a long, tough regimen of training and mental torment, but it was a challenge I had no choice but to take on. Graham had fought all of my battles for me up until this point, but that option was no more. I could only imagine what skullduggery he would be up to without me, the loss of him ever present now in my life. The thought of me fighting, to this day, still a daunting one to my puny, exercise-free body. I have to give myself some credit here. My monumental boxing career lasted some three weeks. More accurately, twenty-one days, a split lip, and a broken nose. Fuck Rocky; even he didn't take this much punishment and abuse. And I did learn a valuable lesson about getting too involved in action movies for the future. I still left the cinema ready to take on the world, but I made sure the world didn't physically want to take me on.

It was the middle of the summer holiday; what to do now? No more best friend, no more boxing career. I think I needed another *outlet* for my anger, or complete boredom more like, whichever way you choose to look at it. School summer holidays were always greatly looked forward to, but also always greatly overrated. With the endless weeks of spare time drawing to an end, and with my mother's daily suggestions fast running out, I was reduced to wandering the streets alone, without

Graham, my forbidden friend, listlessly throwing rocks at passing cars' windshields.

Then, one day as if back in the boxing ring, I was punched again by a thumping great idea—my next genius money-making venture. My parents actually encouraged this vocation. After several viewings of *The Karate Kid* at the local cinema (alone, of course), the brilliant "Wax-On-Wax-Off" car washing scheme was conjured up and subsequently birthed. A gem of an idea, even if I do say so myself. On the weekends I would borrow my next-door neighbor's karate outfit, yellow belt (not as cool as Daniel's and Miyagi's black belt, but I was a beginner after all), take my bucket of soapy water and tattered sponge, and plead with the surrounding neighborhood to let me wash their cars as a part of my karate *Miyagido* training. What better way to help keep an annoying kid off the street than make him work? This all went surprisingly well. Swimmingly well, in fact. At the end of the summer I was earning money, and I was seriously training in karate as described in detail by Mr. Miyagi. And besides, the white suit was looking pretty fantastic on me.

Inevitably, with every great idea there is the proverbial spanner that is thrown into the works. The beauty of British weather is that it can go from a heat wave to arctic conditions in a day. The freezing, bitterly cold finale of the summer holidays soon put an abrupt end to my training to be the next Karate Kid. It really wasn't my fault—the weather was never a problem for Daniel and Miyagi in California. As it got colder, my hands cracked and split, bleeding into the harsh water, and the karate suit provided very little (and I say this with generosity), protection from the freezing elements.

Watching the film over and over again had sparked something in me, though. I had found a great moneymaking idea, and also the ultimate girlfriend in Elizabeth Shue (California-blonde-perky-girl-with-money). It's not actually right to call her my girlfriend, because she really had absolutely no input in—or even any idea of—the decision to be involved with me, or our imaginary cooked-up relationship. The flickering celluloid of the *Rocky* films and subsequently *The Karate Kid* had adopted me, placed me into Elizabeth Shue's care, and led me away from the park, a life of crime, and my best friend, but ultimately I had come full circle back to the safety of the cinema. And then it dawned on me—the missing link in my life. The reason none of the summer really seemed to matter. The one magic detail, a forbidden friend with whom to share my schemes and the cinema and, of course, to discuss my new soon-to-be girlfriend. Why didn't I just reacquaint myself with Graham Tonkin and not tell my mother? She would never have to know of our blossoming partnership again. Could the solution really be that simple?

Absolutely. Why not?

CHAPTER ELEVEN

❧

THE AMITYVILLE HORROR, 1979

Directed by Stuart Rosenberg.
Based on a true story by writer Jay Anson, The Amityville Horror is
about a large house on the coast of Long Island where newlyweds George
(James Brolin) and Kathy Lutz (Margot Kidder) and their three children
move into their dream home. Not aware that a murder took place in the
house several years before, the new owners turn to their family priest for
help in ridding their home of evil spirits. The priest performs an exorcism
on the house to cleanse it of its unwanted inhabitants.

Throughout my life I have tortured myself by watching certain films over and over again purely for the thrill of being terrified. *The Amityville Horror, A Nightmare on Elm Street, Psycho, Carrie, The Exorcist, Halloween,* and *Poltergeist* were all very dodgy films for a kid to be sat in front of, but films that every kid *has* sat in front of. There was always the distinct possibility that seeing these types of movies as a child could turn you into a person liable to break into little bits upon seeing a priest clutching a Bible or if you witnessed another child place their hands on a television screen. Certain films cause universal reactions no matter where in the world you were born or bred. If you have seen *Jaws*, you have done the bloody music while flailing around in the ocean. It's a 100 percent certainty. And if you're as stupid as I was, you have attacked your unsuspecting family members with the double whammy—the stupid music *and* your arm stuck vertically out of the water replicating the fin, cunningly disguised as an arm (and just as deadly).

The supposed age restrictions cinemas try to enforce to keep children out of public showings of horror films in fact only serve to fuck kids up even more. It's a FACT. Children, if told

78

by any form of authority not to watch something, will soon become overwhelmed with the desire to watch the now-forbidden spectacle. Instead of watching cinematic horrors safely surrounded by numerous people from within the confines of the comforting cinema walls, children are reduced to watching them with a brave accomplice at a late-night viewing at a mate's house. Very much alone. The slightest movement and ensuing sounds from the house would cause heads to snap violently and simultaneously in the direction of the eerie noise.

Horror films, in my case, would begin to unspool usually around my now-prohibited yet still-very-much-available friend, Graham, and his spooky abode. Shortly after the commencement of the wobbly Betamax video, Graham inevitably would start to suck his thumb and I would act as though I didn't notice. This act was never brought up in conversation—it just didn't need to be. We loved to be terrified by these films and we clung to all the comfort we could, no matter how infantile it was outside these walls, just as long as our secrets stayed inside the structure.

My parents soon became aware of my reacquaintance with Graham and caught wind of the highly illegal schemes we concocted as we huddled nightly, trying not to give each other horror film–induced heart attacks. Swiftly and without warning, they decided to take some drastic, scary action of their own. They made a quite rash decision to sell everything they owned and move the entire family to a more secluded part of England, the Cambridgeshire countryside. The most exciting thing happening in this part of the country was crop rotation in the surrounding fields, which tended to draw a healthy crowd at the appropriate time of the year. Were they having a laugh? Every member of my family was to be ripped from the only thing they had ever known due to my apparent behavioral problems? Of course, I hated them for it, which in turn made my behavior take a sudden turn for the worse. I took a last stand fighting to the very end as the professional moving men carried out furniture to a waiting truck, refusing to leave the comfort of my bed as they removed the objects around me. They would have to carry me out, pajamas on display for the whole of South London to see. Which, with great amusement, they willingly did.

Due to the fact that nobody in their right mind would ever want to move to the desolate place we were headed for in the east of England, houses were big, cheap, and in plentiful supply. The house my parents bought was quite a *steal* which, oddly, was the deed that had brought us here in the first place. My parents had purchased a house with the auspicious name of "Ramsey Manor," a homestead so old it had been listed in the historic Norman *Domesday Book*. Following England's invasion by William of Normandy in 1066, he set about recording how much each landowner held in land and livestock, and what its worth and location were. In my mind the house that I would struggle to call home probably wasn't worth much more than its original listing more than 900 years ago. It was cold, damp, and created a foreboding outline against the crisp night sky. It was very similar to the *Psycho* house, four stories high and with a definite voice of its own, creaking and cracking as it swayed nightly in the cold eastern winds. My bedroom was to be located in the old servants' quarters at the very top of the house, where mischief was less likely to come searching for me as we all tried our hardest to settle into a very different life.

To help fill the void in the house and, more importantly,

the void in my parents' new, quieter life, they were soon to adopt a couple of baby girls, fearful that their days of parenting were coming to a slightly bumpy end. They named them the decidedly normal names of Amy and Georgina, a convention finally learned from the lessons of torment that my brother and I had endured while in the English educational system. I believe my parents were afraid of the prospect of having time to do the *things* everyone talks longingly about doing when you reach a certain age—they just didn't know what those *things* were. After spending the last sixteen years taking care of children, they continued on, safely doing the *thing* they new best. The days and nights in our house were once again filled with the sounds of inquisitive children, but another presence was also about to make itself known.

As we slept at night the voice of our new homestead grew louder and increasingly more perplexing. From where I rested high above the ground floor, doors could be heard shutting and stairs being walked upon at all hours of the night. Try as I could to justify or find any kind of rational reason for the sounds that disturbed my slumber, there was no apparent reason to uncover. And as time moved on, the noises became increasingly brazen.

My mother was once awakened in the dead of night by a strange sound—the rustling of a stiff taffeta dress as it was being fitted onto its owner. A ball could be heard bouncing, followed by the patter of children's playful feet, on the ceiling above us when, as a family, we sat down to dinner. A woman could be heard sighing from various places in the house, and most disturbing of all, my two new adopted sisters began to complain about the old lady standing at the foot of their beds, staring at them in the middle of the night. Welcome to the family, girls; I hope you enjoy the ride.

While watching most horror films you usually begin to wonder why, when the bizarre occurrences happen, the family doesn't run from the house screaming and flailing their arms. You would think that a situation such as blood in the toilet or whispering voices telling you to leave would be quite a clear indicator of your subsequent actions. But, as in the most classic of horror movies, my family chose to stay, putting it all down to weird dreams and the noise of the wind. Collectively, however, we all knew this was a grandiose concoction of a lie. Let the ensuing terror begin—was all this still some sort of bizarre punishment for stealing some BMX stickers? I wouldn't put it past them.

This area of England was totally miserable to me in every possible sense of the word. It was the polar opposite of the place where my life had blossomed years earlier. I knew not one soul in the surrounding area, and even if I had, there was very little to do in the form of entertainment. I soon found solace in the confines of my bedroom studying any and every film I could lay my hands upon, as if each was created by a great artistic master with a varied and inspiring palette. I had sunk into a heightened state of melancholy—even comedies didn't seem in the slightest bit amusing to me any more. Could it be true? Had Steve Guttenberg really lost his golden touch? What's not to love about *Police Academy?*

One dark winter's night I lay huddled in my enveloping sheets, illuminated only by the random flickers emanating from the television screen. It had reached that hour, the time where sleep became the vehicle by which days bled seamlessly into one another. I closed my eyes and slowly drifted off into a deep warm sleep, with a creeping feeling of nostalgia for my previous life in London already settling in.

Suddenly, in the middle of the night, a loud sigh was breathed directly into my ear as if someone or something had their lips pressed against my head. My eyes opened with ferocity, dilating to the size of saucers, pulling me harshly and relentlessly from my night's sleep. Every hair on my body was erect; goosebumps were puckering my skin. I was totally unable to move. I was in a state of complete and utter terror like I had never experienced before. My breathing quickened, leaving a trail of vapor in the now-freezing room. I wanted desperately to perform a simple bodily action and turn myself onto my other side, but my limbs wouldn't even consider comprehending. I knew there was something else in my bedroom with me but I was frozen in position, completely disabled by fear. All of my senses were now acutely awake, and the only sound I could make out was that of my panicked breath.

And then *she* appeared.

The woman walked straight through my locked bedroom door with a familiar authority. I wanted to vocalize my fears in some form but my throat felt so restricted that no discernible sound left my mouth. I began to sweat profusely. Why had she awakened me from my nights' sleep? I could only imagine the worst. Her long, white gown was trimmed with lace and looked more like nighttime attire than any sort of dress or uniform. She was quite obviously from another time and place in history. She moved in a fluid movement yet was slightly translucent, the familiar objects of my room still quite visible through her figure. As the woman turned in my direction, her eyes paused as if staring at a spot directly above me. Her hair was pulled back from her middle-aged face, and she seemed troubled yet determined. The lady, as if brought back from a deep thought whence her mind had drifted, made a swift movement toward my petrified body, walking straight through my legs, causing my sweating body to shudder with a sudden and harsh chill. She was now out of my sight but very much still in the cold room. I knew I had to turn over to watch her no matter what it took or what it could in turn provoke. Although the fear was intense, I was very much aware of the rarity of the vision before me and understood it was not to be wasted. As if squeezing my body from the confines of the heaviest boulder perched upon my chest, I managed to rotate to the strange sight of the lady with her forearms in the wall, elbow-deep. She withdrew her limbs, straightened her gown, and walked back through me, disappearing again into her own world, oblivious to my presence. Or was she? After all, it was she who had awakened me to witness this baffling, terrifying sight.

If there was one thing that would solidify in my mind escaping the confines of my new home I think this occurrence would be it. The deal was signed, sealed, and delivered by a translucent bird. Take your industrious forearms and terrify some other unsuspecting bugger. I had reached the peak of my terror. I NEEDED to move back to London and I would have gladly run all the way there, screaming and flailing my arms behind me at the slightest opportunity, breaking the mold of the most traditional horror films, thank you very much.

This woman was clearly a troubled soul. But why was she continuing about her daily routine hundreds of years after she had physically left this earth? And more importantly, get your pasty forearms out of my wall, you cheeky girl!

Upon further research into the house and its history, many new details were uncovered—information conveniently not passed on to my parents by the real estate agents when Mum and Dad purchased our new home. At some point in its historic timeline, the auspicious Ramsey Manor, our new and entertaining homestead had been the site of a fatal house fire. As was customary back in those days, the doors of the children's bedrooms were locked by their guardians to ensure a sound night's sleep for the entire household. Unfortunately, the children in Ramsey Manor had perished in the blaze, leaving the guilt to be carried on by the servant, the so-called *pasty lady* now disturbing me with her sighs, missing forearms, and general tomfoolery. But what to make of those limbs in the wall? What was all that mucking about? My bedroom, at a later date of remodeling, would uncover a secret of its own. Behind the wall, unbeknownst to anyone, was a very old fireplace from around the same time period as the fire. It had long since been bricked up and discarded. It was here that the servant ghost carried on her duties at the fireplace, still quite diligent, now tending to the new children in the house, positioned at the foot of our beds looking down upon us.

I couldn't stay here in this new home, I made a promise to myself. I could barely set foot inside my room again, even in the brightest of light. Everything I thought about was back in London. Or was I just trying to escape back to a more innocent time of my childhood? A vicious struggle ensued with my parents that would keep me from returning to London for many arduous years. London was not within their life's plan for me. After all, this uprooting of the family in their mind was not an act carried out in vain.

By the time I arrived back in London, having escaped my teenage years and rural environment, living again a few doors down on the very same street that I had grown up on, and lodging now with my senile grandmother, everything had altered. Life had not innocently waited for my return; it had moved on rapidly around me, and the most familiar of surroundings were themselves now a strange land. Friends had grown up, and they had jobs, families, and responsibilities. The place I had struggled to get back to for so many years was not the place of my childhood at all; it was now just the dirty streets of Croydon I saw everyone else trying desperately to escape from. On my journeys to London on the train, I began to withdraw and avoid eye contact at all costs with people I had known for the entirety of my life. Something was VERY wrong. I had strayed from my life's path and needed to refocus the route upon which I would happily walk down. Surely I owed myself happiness and a purpose. This wasn't at all how it was meant to be.

CHAPTER TWELVE

>

BATMAN FOREVER, 1995

Directed by Joel Schumacher.
Batman (Val Kilmer), Two-Face (Tommy Lee Jones), and The Riddler
(Jim Carrey) star in the third film of the Batman series. The film
thunders along in the Batmobile, Batwing, and Batboat with a generic
good vs. evil story line. For the first time in the franchise, Batman
acquires a partner, Robin (Chris O'Donnell), to help the caped crusader
battle the Gotham City underworld.

At the conclusion of my senior school education, my father began to bestow upon me the inevitable—career advice. When I expressed the desire to work in film, he cautiously advised me to have a safety net, one which would provide financial stability if my acting dream didn't fully materialize. During the eighties the two highest-paid career fields were either in advertising or in aviation. Due to my fear of heights, this essentially left me with merely one viable option for my safety net. Whether I was actually even slightly talented in this field didn't even cross my mind as I set out on what seemed like a huge diversion from where my passion lay. It would eventually take me nearly five long years to complete my studies in advertising and graphic design, but that's another story in itself. Upon completion of college, I methodically once more pursued my true aspiration in the city of London—making a living acting in the film industry I so adored.

I sat precariously on London's filthy underground, traveling at jerky intervals as I passed the Tottenham Court Road station in the closing hours of the day. The stale smell of urine and alcohol-laced vomit seemed to hang in the air from every corner, seeping into the fibers of my clothes and penetrating the pores of my skin. The mess seemed endless, being fruitlessly mopped from the floor by disenchanted station workers with their yellow buckets of disinfectant. The acting class I was taking in the heart of the city had become a regular weekly commitment and, most importantly, it paved the way for a new, positive direction on my own personal character arc. To continue my studying after class ended, I would closely watch the mixture of people that frequented the station late at night. It was here you could find a wealth of characters that could be adapted into stage performance, hidden between the circular, tiled walls of the tube.

It was an unusually cold night in London as I sat on the train listening to a private conversation I had no business eavesdropping on. I was obviously trying my best to look as disinterested as I could in the unfolding story the two men told. With childlike enthusiasm, a father whispered about a secret audition that his son had attended during the day. Apparently, the infamous Hollywood director John Macher was in town looking at "talented yet unknown actors" to play the role of a superhero sidekick in an upcoming major comic book film adaptation.

You may find yourself at this juncture not being too familiar with John Macher's fine body of work. This is quite possibly because his name in this context is entirely concocted. This pseudonym has been fabricated by the author for simple legal reasons—to conceal the actual filmmaker's name, which, in time, the need for which will become apparent. Therefore, "John Macher" will be playing the part of the real-life director described within the subsequent story, which I will now proceed to tell.

The information stolen from the overheard conversation was all I needed. I had been struck with a brilliant idea—a germ which had quickly materialized and lodged itself in my head, and there would be no way to rid myself of it unless I followed it through to the bitter end.

I would be cast as the next superhero sidekick in an upcoming major comic book film adaptation.

This was my destiny, my fate—or at least that is what I quickly convinced myself. I was absolutely certain I could pull off the yellow tights (adorned with red underpants discretely positioned on the outside so the general public could ascertain my superhero status). But where on earth could I find Mr. Macher to convince him to relinquish his futile search?

The night left me feverish with schemes, and after the little sleep I had obtained, I set out on my newfound superhero mission the very next day. I began diligently to make phone calls, pursuing everyone even remotely involved with the film business. Film magazines, newspapers, the local video shop, even Barry Norman's office (the telly's resident film critic) trying to find out where the director was residing, but to no avail. They all denied knowledge of him even being in the country, using the most condescending of paparazzi lines: "Trust me, son, we would know if he was here. Hollywood doesn't come to London unless we're there to welcome them at the airport." Could these muppets be any less helpful? Then, in my failing desperate state, a stroke of superhero genius struck.

I placed a call to Warner Bros. in-development department telling them I was from a courier company and I needed to verify the casting director's address for the upcoming superhero project. I knew they would never give out the director's address, but the location of the casting director was a more attainable proposition, and one they would reluctantly relinquish—I mean why wouldn't they? I thought I finally had them in my gloved supergrasp. My quest was coming to an end; my big Hollywood break was about to materialize.

Victory was mine—I finally had in my possession an address but, more importantly, now I had another name associated with the project, a name that would soon know my name. I excitedly called the casting director, Lucy, asking her if I could present my picture to her for the young superhero role. To my pleasant surprise she was quite receptive and polite, curious as to how I'd found out about the role without any kind of top agent involvement, but nevertheless still very cordial. Within the hour my best crime-fighting head shot was being whisked over by motorcycle courier to the other side of London, and so I patiently waited for my first big audition time to be scheduled, my diary and pen close at hand.

I waited...

And waited...

No call. In fact, no tinkling of the superhero phone whatsoever. I couldn't stand it a minute longer. Bloody hell—fucking courier companies. If you want something done you have to do it yourself. I grabbed the phone and called them to see if they had received my package.

THE FIRST BIG MISTAKE

I had now been relegated to talking to the casting director's assistant. Lucy, it seemed, was now too busy to take my call. It was her assistant's job to inform me in an overly exaggerated tone of disappointment that I "looked adorable, but there was just no audition spaces to see me at this time." Adorable…what exactly does that mean? Did I look like a sodding puppy in my photograph? The director was allegedly already meeting his favorite actors for the role on second auditions and had a very tight schedule for the next few days. She hurriedly thanked me for my enthusiasm and informed me they would keep me in mind for their upcoming projects, hanging up the phone before any kind of discernible response could leave my mouth. NO THANKS! What was she talking about? Future projects. Didn't these people have X-ray vision? How could they be so blind? They couldn't turn me down, could they? That wasn't even an option. I was destined for this. Why couldn't they see this? Maybe I just actually had to show them. If that was the route they wanted us to go down, then Plan B needed to go into effect. This plan was also commonly known as the Drop and Leg It Maneuver.

THE SECOND BIG MISTAKE

How they underestimated me. A crime fighter never gives up until the job is done and the bird has been saved. The next day I called Warner Bros. once more and found out the name of the film company's chaperone assistant who was looking after John Macher while he stayed in the city. I knew getting this information was a long shot, but I figured I just had to have authority in my voice and take no shit from the corporate bastards. Looking back now, I am quite convinced I could have had the guy from Warner's sign his life savings over to me—he was that receptive. I used the cunning mind trick of placing the call first thing in the morning, a time when people have just arrived for work and don't want aggravation from a tosser like

91

me to start their day with. Mornings were always the very best time, I have found, to gain any kind of insider knowledge. The idea was to get in and out before the breakfast coffee has touched their lips.

Having the director's assistant's name in my possession now as well, I called the casting director back, disguising my voice as best as possible.

"Lucy, how are you? I just had breakfast with our good friend John Macher, and he accidentally left his jacket in the restaurant, the silly boy that he was. I'm sure he must have a million things on his mind right now. John told me that he was meeting with the casting people today and asked if I could drop it directly off at his hotel as he didn't need it for the rest of the morning. Silly me hung up before asking John which hotel he was staying at this time around. I don't want to call him back and bother him again as he's not in the greatest of moods, so I was wondering if by chance you knew where…"

"Claridges," the assistant rapidly replied.

"Of course he is, that's right…his usual haunt. How silly of me." I thanked her profusely and hung up the receiver, my face beaming with the equalizing goal in our battle of wills.

You naive girl, didn't your mother inform you to never talk to strange boys? The information and trust you receive from people never ceases to amaze me. Nobody apart from a select few knew he was in the country, but now that select few included yours truly. He would be mine. Look out John Macher—get ready for a personal viewing of my silky cape and underpants, oh yes!

I was on a high, my fibs now knew no bounds. My next call was to the ever-helpful, overly posh Claridges Hotel, this time in a dodgy *Dukes of Hazard* American accent.

"Y'all have a friend of mine, John Macher, staying with you, and it's his birthday this week. A few of his closest friends are going to surprise him in the morning, and I was wondering what his normal schedule was like there? You see, we wanted to arrange a champagne breakfast for him."

"What a delightful idea sir, and may I say how thoughtful his friends are. Mr. Macher normally jogs around 8:00 before his breakfast at 8:30."

"Thank you very much, you've been a great help. You're a real credit to the hotel. Your discretion in this matter would be greatly appreciated, of course."

"Absolutely, sir," he replied, as if the posh twat were winking at me on the other end of the line. *Click* went the receiver. Tomorrow Hollywood hotshot Mr. Macher would be mine.

THE THIRD BIG MISTAKE

Recalling the events with the perfect clarity of hindsight, I even begin to scare myself. Can you say John Lennon or *Catcher in the Rye*? But at the time, everything seemed strangely normal and even quite justified, and besides, by this point it had become a battle of persistence. That evening I put together my package. It included my head shot and résumé and a letter proving to the director that I had a superhero sidekick's mentality, having pieced together all the clues to find him, so to please at least audition me. I finally put my years of art school training to good use, using computer technology to its full potential, scanning in the Warner Bros. logo and creating some fake yet very official looking envelopes and ID badges. I got up at six the next morning ready to amaze and impress this mere mortal, and I was loitering outside his hotel by 7:30. I was dressed in an official looking, formal business suit, but as a beautiful extra little treat for him, I had a very authentic rented superhero costume on underneath it so he could see how good I looked in tights. As I stood in front of this swanky hotel, something pretty important dawned on me. I had no fucking clue what John Macher looked like. How would I know it was him? Could I really be this much of a retard?

As people jogged by me in the early hours of London's new, awakening day, I couldn't help but stare into their eyes, committing each to memory. Sure enough, as I was to find out later, the director did jog past me in one of those slow-motion moments. His eyes locked with mine, twice, in a mysterious, apprehensive gaze. The rumble in London's jungle was about to happen.

The time was 8:35. I approached the front desk, heart racing, my sweaty palms clutching the envelope as tightly as I could, as if it contained my soul.

"Hi, I'm from Warner Bros. I have a very important package for Mr. Macher. Would you be so kind as to let him know I'm here?"

They tried aimlessly to pry the package from me at the desk, but I informed them it was highly classified material and had to be delivered into Mr. Macher's hands directly. They called up to John's room explaining the situation and he told them to send me right up, of course—why wouldn't he?—thinking Warner Bros. had something urgent for him.

Haaaahhhaaaaaaaaaaaaaaaaa!

The lift operator tried to make polite conversation but I was in no mood. I was a man on a mission. The big hit was about to take place. The old lift came to a jolting stop and I collected myself, delicately adjusting my hair, stalling with a couple of deep breaths before calmly stepping out onto John's floor. The lift doors shut gently behind me—I kept walking. The tie, shirt, and jacket came off. I kept walking. The silky tights were straightened. My walking quickened. My superhero package was properly adjusted. I had reached my destination, I was standing in front of his room door, cape billowing behind me, now having massive second thoughts about this whole ridiculous scheme. What the fuck was I thinking? Paranoia had swept over me. I looked quickly in every direction. Were cameras watching me? Could I really have struggled to take my trousers off without them realizing there was something not quite kosher going on with the Warner's special delivery? JUST DO THE DROP!

I knocked on his door, package in hand. Oh shit...where's my eye mask? The door slowly opened revealing the great American film director John Macher who had quite obviously just stepped from the great English shower decked out in a bathrobe, a towel drying his long strands of grey hair. Ah...maybe this wasn't the right time for this kind of business? Then John made a motion to speak, but left a pause so big you could have driven a train through it.

"You're from Warner Bros.?" he said staring at my half-arsed costume.

"NO...not exactly," I replied, trying to sound as confident as possible in my actions.

It was then that I witnessed his face drop, so much so that I thought I would be picking his nostrils up off the floor. Plain and simple (rightly so, of course), the man was in total shock. I saw his life flashing rapidly past him, his eyes flickering as he made the connection between me, Mr. Shifty standing outside the hotel in a dodgy suit, to me now, a maniacal caped crusader. It was obviously time to bail out and quickly…but the speech, the speech!

"I know quite obviously this is probably a bad time to ask but I really want you to audition me for the role I am so perfect my number is in the package so you can call me when you've finished your hair and as you can see I look really good in tights," I blurted out in a stream of consciousness without pause or hesitation.

Still not one word from Mr. Macher. He just kept nodding his head slowly as I blabbed on—the words pouring from me as he searched for a pause. I think some serious bad timing all round was at work here. John quite obviously wasn't ready for me to amaze him at such an early hour, and I was later to find out he had just completed a movie about an ordinary man that goes on a killing rampage, which still was understandably in the forefront of his mind.

"I'll…er, take a look," he quietly mumbled, his movements lethargic and unsure.

I thanked him, thrust the package into his now-trembling hand, and made a quick exit, flying down the stairs past those helpful receptionists, my cape billowing behind me as I exited into the cold early morning London street.

As the day progressed I did actually receive that call that I had been so impatiently awaiting from the casting director. But not quite the one I had hoped for. I was informed John had been so disturbed and upset that someone could get so close to him in London that he had left the country that very morning on the first plane out back to America, absolutely furious and vowing never to return to England again. The casting assistant who had so kindly given me the information I requested had lost her job, and England's top casting director told me she would do everything in her power to make sure I would never work as an actor in England again. All in all quite a successful morning for my blossoming thespian career, even if I do say so myself. My film vocation was over in England before I had the opportunity to actually do anything. Shit.

At this juncture, it was time to introduce myself to America. Where else could I go? The land of opportunity where a whole new batch of crimes and misdemeanors were waiting to unfold.

feature presentation...

CHAPTER THIRTEEN

ॐ

COMING TO AMERICA, 1988

Directed by John Landis.
A pampered African prince, Akeem (Eddie Murphy), goes to New York
City to search for the perfect bride. There he breaks the arranged
marriage tradition of his native land, trying to find love on his own terms.
Accompanied by his companion (Arsenio Hall), he quickly finds a new
job, new friends, new enemies...and lots of old-fashioned trouble.

My acting training began in earnest in London, although I had come to realize that it would not be where I professionally worked if a certain casting director had anything to do with it. I had enrolled months before at the Lee Strasberg Acting Institute, but it was obvious—now that I wanted to make a serious career out of acting—that it needed to become something more than a class I attended a few times a week.

Although there was sadly no real film industry in England to speak of, the Lee Strasberg Acting Institute was lucky enough to boast one of America's finest film actresses as its head tutor, Marianna Hill. Marianna was a woman whose résumé shone as radiantly as did her stunning beauty, nightly filling the class with electricity and hope about a career in film as she moved animatedly in front of her students. She told us stories of her experiences alongside Elvis, Al Pacino, and Clint Eastwood, of her friendships with Brando, Cazale, and Strasberg, and I of was transfixed by every second of it. I was an arid sponge that had at last found something, and now someone, to absorb.

I pored over legal papers by day, investigating every possible scenario by which to enter America, while studying my craft by night. Enjoying the fruits that America had to offer for any length of time was not an easy task. With the authorities knowing I had no family or friends I could stay with in America, they were instantly wary. As so many people do, they assumed I would be crossing the border and then disappearing into the vastness, reappearing later to claim poverty and look for financial help from the government. I realistically had one shot at landing in the country and securing work before my money ran out and my ninety-day visitor visa expired.

With my acting teacher's blessing, I boarded my flight to Los Angeles with a round-trip ticket I hoped would go to waste. Failure was not an option I dared to think of. I set out on my journey into a life in film. I settled into my airline seat and made a grab for the transatlantic film schedule. As the feature presentation started on the tiny screen directly in front of me, my mind strayed into what I believed was a perfect metaphor spooling in front of my eyes. I knew I would start out as a small actor in Hollywood, but surely it wouldn't take me long to rise from the small screen, flying to success?

My eyes closed and an innocent smile slowly grew across my face, happy now in the knowledge that opportunity was the only thing waiting to greet me at the airport. Breaking with the traditions of a small town life and the small-minded people I had always been surrounded by, I was determined to find success on my own terms, and I was soon to learn a new way of life, along with, of course, lots of good old-fashioned trouble.

CHAPTER FOURTEEN

૨⁂

BEVERLY HILLS COP, 1984

Directed by Martin Brest.
While investigating the murder of a friend, an unconventional Detroit
cop (Eddie Murphy) finds himself following a lead that lands him in Los
Angeles. There he comes face-to-face with the unique culture of Beverly
Hills. He teams up with two bumbling, reluctant detectives from the Los
Angeles Police Department (Judge Reinhold and John Ashton) who have
been assigned to the case only to keep an eye on him.

There is a scene in the opening of *Beverly Hills Cop* where
Eddie Murphy, much to his amusement, is visually bombarded
by the opulent, over-the-top citizens of Beverly Hills. For
anyone who has ever experienced Beverly Hills, that's pretty
much how it is. Everything is served with a lemon twist. You
find yourself surrounded by people who have way too much
money, illustrating impeccably that money can't buy class. The
fact that some of these citizens have the self-assurance to be
seen in public dressing and behaving the way they do is truly
mind-blowing. Much like Eddie Murphy's character, I had just
arrived in Los Angeles and experienced the same sort of culture
shock. Leaving behind a harsh January storm in England, I was
suddenly thrown into the strange, sunny Californian mix.

In the film, Eddie Murphy's character checked into one of
the most prestigious hotels Los Angeles has to offer. Here is
where our similarities end. I ended up at the less-than-swanky
Hollywood YMCA where I was welcomed by a room with one
cracked window just small enough to prevent a suicide jump,
and a hard wooden board that allegedly doubled as a bed. Not
too different from the police cell standards I had experienced

103

upon outstaying my welcome in Croydon. The initial nights were uncomfortably humid, and the little sleep I managed to obtain was constantly interrupted by the sound of gunfire in the surrounding streets. Buzzing police helicopters chased the bullets, their spotlights highlighting the criminals on the ground. The drone of the flying machines cut into the thick night sky. Welcome to America.

I was soon to discover I was in the midst of a country where, technically, I didn't even exist. No bank account. No driver's license. No employment history. No family. No references. No previous address and therefore no prospect of employment. In my overwhelming desire to reach the shores of the United States, I had overlooked the mechanics of actually existing here. I had arrived wanting desperately to act, thinking naively that surviving here was a certainty.

Time was of the essence due to my entire $1,000 budget slipping daily away, seemingly spending itself and escaping dollar by dollar from the confines of the YMCA. It was at this juncture that I made the first investment in my career. I placed my time and efforts into obtaining fraudulent work papers so that I could at least enter the Hollywood race. The first step naturally in this deceit was uncovering the location of an illegal document ring. Luckily for me, Hollywood's main document ring was so renowned it could have been marked on a tourist map. Within hours I had work papers and identification cards of such good quality even the authorities would have had a hard time deciphering right from wrong. Hearing about good acting jobs or—even more so—the possibility of getting auditions for these good acting jobs would prove to be an infinitely more frustrating task.

·

I knew very little about the specialized skills of movie making, and nothing of the technical terms involved in the process. Quite clearly a crash course in film education was needed. And so arose the opportunity of extra work as a natural vehicle in which to learn all I could about on-set etiquette and terminology.

Extra work is not a healthy thing for any primate to do by any stretch of the imagination, and rest assured there are many monkeys making a career in it. Actors who haven't yet made it, or rather probably wouldn't *ever* make it, in the film world congregate in droves to do extra work. It's easy to get tricked by your own stupidity into feeling like you are a working actor because you are paid to be on a film set. What you fail to see is that you are being paid around $40 a day to be herded around like sheep for hours. Your amazing job is to meander in the background of a scene and be a blurred human form for the camera, which basically any cardboard cutout could do. I succumbed and did a few of these ridiculous jobs before I swore to God I would never subject myself to this modern day form of human torture again. I'm pretty sure if Amnesty International was made aware of the *extra* problem they would drop their programs around the world and focus on this mess. It really was that bad. Bitter, critical, failing actors are the worst kind of people to have to spend a sixteen-hour day with, $40 or not. Believe me.

One evening I was at home and the phone rang, startling the air, breaking the silence with the coarse voice on the other end. "Emmett, I want to check your availability for a film shoot tomorrow," relayed the monotonous voice.

"Sure, I'd love to do it. I'm completely free," came my reflex response, not even pausing for the hint of a breath. I immediately realized my mistake...What was I saying?

"We have a film we would love you to work on. The director has personally selected you from your photograph; he's really eager to get you for the shoot. He said you were just what the production was looking for."

"Will this be extra work?" my voice was now unsure as I ridiculously questioned the owner of an extras casting agency.

"Well, it's only going to be you if that's what you mean; it's not a crowd thing. You will be playing an opponent in a boxing ring. The film is starring, uhh...that uuuhhh...Stallone guy." Still no inflection in her voice, even at this amazing announcement.

That was enough for me. I proudly shared with her that I had endured some boxing training from my youth, and how perfect this job was for me. She definitely had the right athlete for the job.

"I'll do it!" I exclaimed, all initial doubts now knocked from my mind.

And then I was sucker-punched with the fateful question that should have put up a massive red flag, sending me running into the Hollywood Hills. But in my enthusiastic haze it didn't seem at all preposterous at the time.

"You don't have much body hair do you? That's great. The address is..." her monotone voice now picked up with a burst of velocity in the closing of the conversation.

To this day I still don't know why the question of body hair didn't strike me as rather odd. It just didn't. That night I could hardly sleep because of the anticipation; maybe Stallone would let me improvise some dialogue as we boxed. I could add a little

106

English into the mix. "Whoops-a-daisy" could be my catch phrase as I threw out my arms to strike him. The possibilities seemed endless, thoughts racing through my mind with the ferocity of a trained boxing glove piercing the air.

I arose with the first inkling of the sun's rays, beating the dawning day to the initial punch. Excitedly, I caught a bus and then a taxi to the beautiful shooting location—a mansion high in the Hollywood Hills. The huge iron gates opened automatically with a respectful, slow ease as I approached the house. I strolled through the bustling location, everyone happily going about their respective tasks. Each greeted me with a huge, white California smile set from within their tanned faces. Hollywood was opening its sealed, heavy gates and welcoming me in. I had made it, and pretty swiftly too, I assured myself.

The director greeted me with, "Here he is…our guy, great photograph…nice job," extending his hand with a crushing grip as he spoke.

"You're damn right, mate," I replied proudly, my confidence now on a high from the surrounding bustling of activity.

I was led to the boxing ring by the director, which at the time was filled with a couple of saucy blonde wrestling sisters rehearsing something. The anorexic twins complete in their patriotic, or should I say idiotic, tiny stars-and-stripes sequined bikinis. Wow, God bless America.

I was informed that my moment of glory wasn't going to be until the afternoon due to unforeseen circumstances, so I should just relax by the huge pool and enjoy the California sun. Now that I could do. All in all a great start to the day.

That morning by the water I met the strangest group of people I think have ever been assembled for a motion picture. The wrestler-now-turned-actor Rowdy Roddy Piper, a nice bloke with a dodgy kilt, but you can't really trust a man who introduces himself as Rowdy Roddy with a straight face. Joey Butafucco, straight from his very talented role in the Amy Fisher story, and a strange giant bald man from the horror film *The Hills Have Eyes*. Sylvester Stallone's brother Frank was also poolside feigning importance, quite obviously Sly's assistant, I assumed.

We sat around the enticing pool of water staring at the reflections of one another, wondering how we were all meant to weave together within this most bizarre of stories. With nothing to do for the entire day, I made good use of my time by stuffing my face with the free food offered.

The place for all imaginable shit food on a film set has the very upscale name "The Craft Service Table," which sounds a lot nicer than it actually is. There is no *craft* in the pre-packed food preparation, and no *service* to be offered in presenting the food to you, but there is normally a table involved, so it gets by without being a total lie. The craft service area is normally a nightmare for the health-conscious, figure-watching actor, but for me that meant nothing but a breakfast of jam donuts, chocolate, and the essential red licorice. Licorice was the adult equivalent of having popcorn when seeing a movie as a kid. I came to discover that you are guaranteed to find and desire this strange, red treat on any movie set no matter where you are in the world. This set was no exception.

I got a hold of a copy of the script in an attempt to uncover my scene with the elusive Mr. Stallone. I flipped through the pages several times to no avail. Strangely, he himself only had a couple of scenes, mainly fighting with the two blonde idiots I had witnessed preparing earlier. Obviously, this was one of those star cameos. Sylvester Stallone, much like myself, wasn't going to be utilized to his full potential. Maybe another story line had been added at the last minute in a much later version of the script. Yes, that must have been it. I could only hope.

It was getting close now for my big moment of Hollywood screen time, the new golden age of cinema dawning. We had been given a half-hour warning before I was to be placed in front of the camera lens, and I entered the makeup room ready so my face looked its very best. The makeup girls seemed really insistent and very strict about my lack of body hair, sharing the casting director's strange requirement. Maybe the shot would be such an extreme close-up that every follicle would show?

My armpits were shaved, stubble was scrubbed clean from my neck, my nipples plucked, and my chest waxed. I thought they were taking this a little far. I was going to look like a total nancy boy by the time they were finished. My perplexed questions were met with a smile as if I was pulling their leg, and still no one discussed the scene with me. My legs were shaved and my pubic hair neatly trimmed. Still no word. The only indicator as to what lay ahead was that I was now being referred to as the "Stunt Guy" on the set. At last, a time to prove my masculinity to the world…but with plucked nipples? Now the finishing touch, the proverbial cherry on top. I was ready for the costume fitting.

I was steadily going through my method actor's routine as I walked to the wardrobe department, my years of theater training in London finally put into practice. I needed to be calm, I needed to be focused, I needed to remember to breathe. The costume girl, as with everyone else, had an enormous smile on her face as I entered the room. She looked me slowly up and down swallowing her grin before hesitantly moving toward the overflowing clothes rack to pull my costume. What would best accentuate my talents? Would it be a silk boxing robe, the English Stallion vs. the Italian Stallion?

To my utter horror what she reached for was the smallest bikini imaginable. A string bikini which was pretty much just string, identical to the ones worn by the blonde idiots I had seen earlier...except for one special, added bonus. A pair of huge fake rubber breasts were firmly attached to the inside of the bikini top. I stood there motionless. Was she having a fucking laugh at my expense? Was she just being friendly and showing me one of the other ridiculous birds' costumes from the movie? Please, God, tell me she was. She had to be!

"You can slip it on in that changing room there," a wry grin quivering from the corners of her mouth. My face crumpled in horror, contorting in utter confusion. How could I politely say to her, "Why don't you go fuck yourself costume bird? I'm a serious English actor, not some sort of rubber tit!"

For a moment I seriously considered just walking away, at least telling her she was as mad as a badger if she thought I was going to ridicule myself on film (which was tantamount to eternal ridicule). I was beginning to flail in complete and utter panic about the rapidly declining state of what I believed to be my first starring role.

"Great, thanks a lot...Should I use the women's or men's changing room?" I managed to utter that afternoon as I clasped helplessly for my last shred of dignity.

Walking from the costume room to the set was an extremely long, slow walk. Adjusting to the weight of my mammaries, it was a modern-day transvestite death march. My pride was about to be slaughtered for the masses to view. Every single person I passed felt obliged to whistle at my breasts or make some hilarious comment. Would the comedy never end? At this point, you may be asking yourself what the scope of this strange acting role was and what, pray tell, great film it was to be in. The scene was designed to film a joke where a *friend* of Frank Stallone (that would be Sly's brother's friend) uses my enormous, patriotic, plastic breasts as a punching bag while prancing around in the ring.

Of course, now it all made perfect sense! By the laws of reason you can't punch a woman's breasts for entertainment's sake. Hitting my rubber tits in front of the camera was a whole different story. If I was to die quickly, my life flashing before my eyes, one of the key images would be my time in the center of a boxing ring. Me and my huge, rubber breasts bouncing (nipples slightly erect) as I ran from the onslaught of punches. The scene was as well documented as anything I have ever seen on a movie set. Random people pulling cameras from various orifices to capture this moment of ridicule. Everyone acting as if this was something distantly related to the film's production. Take after take. My breasts deflating from the sequined bikini, with what little was left of my ego.

Finally the shot was done, the sadistic party satisfied with the amount of torture I had endured. Graciously, the crew gave me a huge round of applause, some taking it a little too far as I stepped from the ring, making a grab for my bottom on the way back to my dressing room. How could I be so stupid? I swore to

God never again would I compromise my years of serious method acting training with extra work. My teachers would be horrified if they could see me in that bikini; it wasn't even my color! I'm pretty damn sure that Brando or James Dean didn't start like this. Never again would I work for such pathetic wages, and be totally unaware of what I was getting myself into. Never again would I set my acting standards so low.

I would hold my ground with dignity for a couple of weeks until the prospect of a crisp $40 and another cracker of a job came my way.

Pathetic.

CHAPTER FIFTEEN

ॐ

FOUR WEDDINGS AND A FUNERAL, 1994

Directed by Mike Newell.
The film follows the fortunes of Charles (Hugh Grant) and his friends as
they ponder if they will ever find true love and get married. Carrie
(Andie McDowell) plays the token American thrown into this British
farce. The group find themselves attending four weddings and a funeral.
Nominated for an Academy Award for Best Original Screenplay.

There is only so long you can sit and watch the broadcast of the annual Academy Awards without longing to be there yourself. I went to the extent of continually refining my own Oscar speech as the years passed by. When I made the pilgrimage from England to Hollywood, I had brought one tiny, tatty brown suitcase packed with a few personal belongings, ready to start my new life across the pond. You can be sure, though, that in the extremely limited amount of space the luggage provided me, I had found enough room for my tuxedo. Just in case the red carpet swiftly beckoned me to stand upon its shag pile.

My tuxedo had only been exposed to the world a mere four times: once at a friend's nuptials and the subsequent three times while crashing a couple of parties at the Cannes film festival. It was not really the most useful item of apparel in a man's wardrobe, but it would soon prove itself most valuable to me upon arriving in the United States. But not in the traditional, conformist way you might think. Having been manufactured from a very coarse and weighty English material, for months the tuxedo had found a new and infinitely more handy use as a blanket. It was my only source of cover from the elements as I slept in the completely-void-of-furnishings flat that I now called home, trying desperately to claw my way up from the accommodation standards set by the YMCA. The extremely limited funds I possessed didn't really cater to buying the highest-thread-count bedding materials, or any type of bed, for that matter. So, my pillow became a rolled up cardigan, my tuxedo jacket the covers, and my mattress was fashioned from the finest of dusty, varnished wooden floorboards.

In stark contrast to the confines of my empty flat, preparations outside my front door for Hollywood's night of lavishness and grandeur were commencing. The annual Academy Awards enlivened the city with a strange energy and buzz. People hurriedly scurrying to and fro, going about their given tasks, gradually building to an outright frenzy on the day of the live television broadcast.

The Academy Awards are actually designated a season in Los Angeles. They are the pinnacle of the awards season, specifically, which is not as ridiculous as it sounds. It's a distinctive season in Hollywood, as the weather would otherwise give you no sense of time or change, being perpetually sunny. Whole television programs are dedicated to possible clothing styles that stars might or might not wear. Rag-trade designers suddenly become big celebrities and press fodder in their own right as they bicker and squabble over the right to dress the new "it" girl. It's also a guarantee that no matter how straight you think you are, whether a star wears champagne taffeta or an off-ivory chiffon dress suddenly becomes very relevant. To absolutely EVERYONE.

Enough was enough. The endless hours of press coverage, overwhelming me like a television tsunami, had driven me into my own jealous frenzy. It was time for me to put my tuxedo to its proper use. The plan was to pick it up off the floor, dust it off, and slide my way into one of the swanky Hollywood Oscar parties.

But how?

The art of gate-crashing a top bash with strict security is actually a lot easier than one would imagine. Attending the Cannes film festival the previous year with a couple of likely London lads, I had evolved the sport of party-ducking into a true art form. My partners in crime for this venture were Simon Tronisec and Saffrazz Buxy. Simon was a lanky comedian with as much hair on his eyebrows as his entire head, and he was the very fortunate son of a multimillionaire. Saffrazz was a wanna-be gangsta rapper, but he was about as ghetto as Prince Charles. Being the only son of a nice, middle-class Pakistani family, Saffrazz was more samosa than street, much to his dismay. They were a pair of top boys and always up for a laugh, no matter how ridiculous or implausible the conceived plan was.

In the south of France we had managed to gain access beyond the velvet rope by using a cunningly simple ploy. Each night the three of us would rotate roles, but we used precisely the same method of entry to the parties. We would stroll out of the tent city of our campsite on the French Riviera every night. We were dolled up like we meant business and followed a few simple rules:

1. Always dress the part. Two of us would dress in black tuxedos and would flank the third who was dressed very Hollywood, or wanky, whichever way you want to look at it. Dark sunglasses in the middle of the night, smoking a fag, a half-opened shirt draped over your body. Always carry as much confidence and bravado as you could muster.

2. Execute a proper limo arrival. We would go toward the general vicinity of the located and confirmed V.I.P. party and proceed to search out one of the fat limo drivers taking a snooze a few streets away while waiting for the return of the actual celebrity they were chauffeuring. These people worked for a pittance. Offering them a twenty to drive you a mere few feet to drop you outside the party entrance was easy money for them. (None of them ever refused. It's a twenty for about sixty seconds' worth of work.) Who wouldn't do it?

3. Bribe the paparazzi. Pretty much the same deal as the limo drivers. Only this time you would palm off another twenty to one of the photographers outside the entrance to the party. Their payment would be for a few flashes of their camera upon your exit from the limo, and the constant calling of your random made-up celebrity name. This action by them would in turn cause a domino effect among their colleagues.

4. Don't act like a tit inside. If you look like you don't belong at the bash, you won't belong for long. (This is the most important of all of the rules.)

It worked like a well-oiled machine every single time. By our third outing, we could even cut out rule number three and save ourselves a twenty. This time the paparazzi really did recognize us, and worked for us of their own accord. We arrived in style, harassed by a swarm of picture-hungry paparazzi sheep, and were quickly directed down into the party. No questions asked. An evening's worth of entertainment and alcohol for the three of us lads, and all for forty quid. Everyone wins. We

116

all go home happy except, of course, the actual celebrities who had to endure our drunken dribble for an entire evening.

Hollywood parties, on the other hand, would surely be a much harder nut to crack. Especially the Oscars, which boasted the granddaddy of all swanky parties. Celebrity is taken so much more seriously and given so much more credibility in this town. People really do know who's supposedly hot and who's not. It's a fact. In Los Angeles even the cashiers working the 3 a.m. shift at the shitty 7-Eleven can tell whether you are an actor of credibility or are just *acting* like you have some sort of credible career. Thus, the old faithful French party plan would need some serious refining.

I would be flying solo on this mission. A stealth bomber of sorts, and I needed first to uncover somebody that I could convincingly pass myself off as for the entire evening. A person whose name would be known, but whose face would still be a complete void in the public's memory. Therefore, nobody would be any the wiser if I stepped into his life for a few hours. Most importantly, though, he would definitely have to be on the guest list at the best V.I.P. party. All-in-all no easy mission.

As luck would have it, 1995 just so happened to be the year of one of the biggest British film comedies of all time in America, *Four Weddings and a Funeral*. This would have to be my ticket, but could I really pass myself off as Hugh Grant? The thought at that juncture in time was not as totally ludicrous as it now sounds. Hugh back then definitely wasn't the recognizable major star he is today. But it would still be very dodgy turf to walk upon, just in case the door girl happened to be a big fan. I couldn't chance it. I needed someone else's identity to borrow for the night, slightly less recognizable but every bit as English…but who could fill this role?

I could only begin to imagine the beautiful women in slinky skintight party dresses that would be gracing such an event, with a gangly English lad between them—yours truly. Surely I could charm them with my European wit, and finish the evening off by taking home a little golden, tanned trophy of my own. Placing her on my mantle...or better yet, bent over the footboard of my bed. Hold up! Who was I trying to kid? It was at this point of my cunning self-trickery that I was reminded of a very astute line from the aforementioned nominated comedy that brought me crashing back to reality. Hugh Grant says to John Hannah's character: "Do you think there really are people who can just go up and say *Hi, babe. Name's Charles. This is your lucky night*"?

"Well, if there are, they're not English," he replies.

Unfortunately, this was as true a line as was ever written. I may not ever be able to pull off that kind of dodgy one-liner, especially at an Oscar party. The thought itself had presented me with something even better, though. A cunning idea. Instead of borrowing the chat-up line, at the very least I could certainly pull off stealing the identity of the genius who wrote the nugget of dialogue. It just so happened he was nominated for an Oscar, so most certainly would be invited to all of the best events. Absolutely perfect. Besides, who the hell knew what the writer Richard Curtis looked like anyway? (Apart from his mother, I'm sure, who might have be able to point him out in a crowd. But then again, it was really doubtful that she would be working the party. And besides the Mrs.-Curtis-as-door-woman scenario, I was willing to take my chances.)

I had no idea how the guest list ordeal would work in this country. Were there tickets to the event, or did you just arrive and present yourself to the red carpet? Well, I could...or possibly…but what if…FUCK IT. Why not just cut to the chase. Call the venue directly, pose as Richard Curtis's assistant, and get the skinny. Stop faffing around. I ran to the bottom of my street filled with a deceitful excitement, found a working pay phone that would double as my mobile phone (free additional street background noises), and instantly turned myself into assistant to the stars. Man on the move.

"Hello, yes, I was wondering if you could be of assistance. Mr. Richard Curtis's plane has been delayed from London this afternoon so he will be going directly to the Oscar ceremony from the airport. He wanted to make sure he didn't need to rummage through his luggage in the limo, you knows for any kind of invite or identification. The last thing he needs would be an embarrassing scene at the door after his VERY stressful day, as I'm sure you can appreciate," I said in my upper-class English accent to the maître d' in charge of the Oscar party.

"Of course, sir, I totally understand. Mr. Richard Curtis you said?" she responded, very discretely turning the pages of a list as she spoke.

"The very same. I'm sure you are aware of Mr. Curtis's appearance. Just so there's no confusion in spotting him tonight, I'll have him come and make himself known to you at the door. If you could just get him inside as swiftly as possible so as to avoid the paparazzi. I'm afraid they make him terribly nervous. I'm quite certain he would really appreciate it," I said, feeding the accommodating host enough helpful rope to hang herself with.

"Not a problem, sir. I will see to his speedy entrance personally," came her helpful words, spoken through a less-than-discreet smile.

"What did you say your name was again? You have been so

119

incredibly helpful and understanding. I feel your superiors should know how well you perform your job," I said, myself now getting caught up in the obvious pride she took in her work.

"Please, just have him ask for me at the door and I will make sure he is completely taken care of, sir."

She happily gave me her name. The deal was done. Excellent customer service for Mr. Curtis, or for me. Whoever reached the party door first I suppose. All I had to do now was literally wipe the grime from my tuxedo, and introduce it to its fifth good outing. Easy. Surprisingly easy. Could the Americans really be sillier than the French? Is that even possible? That was to be seen, and soon.

As the night rolled on into Academy history, I sat amid the filth on the wooden floor of my flat. I was decked out in full tuxedo jacket, trousers and bow tie topped off with newly polished shoes. I was totally transfixed by the images on my tiny black-and-white television screen, awaiting patiently the chance to step into their colorful world much like Dorothy first landing in Oz. Back then I would normally have about two minutes of good black-and-white TV viewing images. Then a gradual hum would accumulate as if an underground train were approaching from the depths of my telly, destroying the picture in a blizzard of electronic snow, sending me bolting to the antenna clinging on so as not to miss a second of the lavish broadcast.

Unfortunately for Richard Curtis, he didn't take home the Oscar that night for his romantic comedy. Instead, Quentin Tarantino walked away with the prize for *Pulp Fiction*, a fantastic film in its own right. Curtis must have been totally gutted. And to think he wouldn't even be able to drown his sorrows at the after-party bash, as I would be stealing away that prize from him too. This just really wasn't Mr. Curtis's night. I had to hurry.

I jumped onto my bicycle, figuring that due to Los Angeles traffic and added limousine congestion this would be a much faster route. I peddled down the boulevard heading straight for the party. Throngs of gawkers had already congregated seven-deep around the perimeter of the bash, swelling into my vision as I drew near. Movie fans from around the world clamoring to get the briefest glimpse of, or even elusive eye contact with, their chosen pin-up.

While the public was transfixed on the red-carpeted entrance, nobody spotted me pull up behind them all. I stumbled ungracefully from my BMX bike and proceeded to padlock my transportation for the evening to the nearest unmovable object.

As I scouted out the scene, limo drivers could be seen locked in traffic in every direction. None were going to take my measly twenty as bait; that became quickly apparent. The drivers in this town carry as much attitude as the celebrity clientele in their backseats. Think, think, think…fuck it. I'll just walk swiftly and meaningfully toward the door. I ducked behind the crowds, scanning with my peripheral vision for a known big celebrity to ride into the party with. If I could walk closely behind a star, I could steal from them some of the camera flashes. A sly wave to the paparazzi as I passed in front of them would be all it would take, while the famous bods stopped and posed for pictures.

Then it happened. As if a gift was offered down to me from the very heavens above, who should step out of the next limo but the goddess Elizabeth Hurley and on her arm Hugh Grant. It couldn't be more perfect. As they made a beeline for the red carpet and press line, I made my dash for the door. Cameras blazed around me, illuminating the night sky, all of them pointed, obviously, directly at Hugh and Liz. I slipped in front of them for the briefest of seconds, like a well-choreographed dance move. Graciously acknowledging the camera bursts, of course, and making sure the people with the coveted list at the door witnessed my every arm elevation. Now to find my contact. The list was gracefully turned from sight as I approached. Just as the first syllables of her name spilt from my lips, a delicate, perfectly manicured woman's hand extended toward me, offering a familiarly helpful voice.

"Mr. Curtis, congratulations on your nomination. Right this way, sir."

Wow, it was like child's play. I was in the inner Oscar sanctum, completely surrounded by celebrity. And for the proverbial cherry on top, just to totally validate my stolen identity, I whispered to the more-than-helpful girl grasping the Who's Who list, "Hugh's on his way in; he's dealing with the press. Total savages. He's so much more accustomed to it than I am."

I gave her a wink, straightened my tatty tuxedo, lifted a champagne flute and a delicate hors d'oeuvre from a passing waiter, and smoothly blended into my night's fun.

Good times.

CHAPTER SIXTEEN

ટ.

RUNNING ON EMPTY, 1988

Directed by Sidney Lumet.
In 1971, Arthur (Judd Hirsch) and Annie Pope (Christine Lahti) blow
up a napalm lab to protest the Vietnam War. Ever since the incident they
have been on the run from the FBI. They chose to live their lives in
hiding, evading the authorities and thus moving their family regularly.
Now their son (River Phoenix) must choose his own life. Possibly the
finest and most underappreciated film by Sidney Lumet.

To really be involved in the acting game, you have to jump
through hoops to find your way into the famed Screen Actors
Guild (SAG). Acceptance cards are coveted among actors like
jewels hidden in *The Maltese Falcon*. You can't even *begin* to
work on decent projects unless you are a part of the union. The
irony is that you can't get into the union until you work on a
decent project. Being a nonunion actor up to this point left me
scraping the bottom of the barrel playing nonunion bit parts.
Or rather, a pair of woman's bits as I now knew about all too
well. There were a number of other oddities unique to
Hollywood that quickly became apparent to me after the time
I had spent here thus far:

1. There are no real seasons in Hollywood (except for
Awards season, of course.) Basically, the sun shines
every single day. The weather forecasters on the news
are more of a formality than any kind of necessity.
Upon the occurrence of any bit of actual weather,
however, the atmospheric drama is heightened to
ridiculous Hollywood levels and plays out on the local

news. The news leads nightly with STORM WATCH! graphics and live reports for the benefit of the terrified masses.

2. People don't leave the cinema after a film has finished here. They wait for the entire length of the credits, reading intensely every last frame. Every citizen of Hollywood has some sort of connection to the film industry. Therefore, even the most subtle of name-droppers patiently wait to affirm their six degrees of separation upon the happy recognition of a name.

3. Oscar parties are catered by the world's top chefs, but the stars don't actually eat anything while there. The food servers constantly circle the mingling, famished throngs like a frustrated plane waiting to land at Heathrow airport. Each actor feasts with their eyes but is ashamed to add a centimeter to his or her waistline.

There are thousands of stories about the lengths people have gone to to gain entry into the elusive SAG. There are certainly enough to fill a book many times over. Each tale about passage into the union is as bizarre and often illegal as another. Mine, of course, was no different on this strange scale. My entry was less of a marathon struggle and more of a bizarre sprint into union rank and file.

The rules, as they stood at the time of my acceptance, involved collecting a handful of union vouchers. For every nonunion job, a select few vouchers were given out amongst hundreds of desperate actors. They were usually distributed by overweight, randy production guys on location, supposedly via a fair and unbiased process, but it was obvious that these men had a fondness for female breasts. But the exposing of my bikinied breasts in movies was now a thing of the past. I obviously needed to seek out another door through which to enter.

Upon arriving in Hollywood, I had littered the town with my head shots, joining every shady acting agency known. For a small fee they would in turn phone me when a suitable job arose. Offering some embarrassingly bad work, of which by this juncture I had done my fair share. In essence you payed them money to get the *chance* to earn money from them (minus another bigger fee deducted from your paycheck if you actually obtained work). I hoped at the very least to recoup my initial investment and took part in their grandiose mafia schemes. In time the phone calls soon began to trickle in from various agencies, but I received one call in particular that was a little more intriguing. I was teased on my answering machine by a booming, rapid-fire voice:

"This is it, Emic. I promised you, didn't I? This job gets you into the union. You know the digits bud. I'm in the office," spoken fluidly as if read from an all-too-familiar agency textbook.

Firstly, I had never spoken with this overconfident assistant before, which would secondly explain him not even knowing how to pronounce my name. My instincts were to just erase the message. To not even deal with Mr. Confidence, but this wouldn't be fair to good old Emic. My alter ego was strangely intrigued with the prospect of union work. Could I really give up my nonunion life of comedy breast roles? I made a swift grab for the phone.

"Emic, how are you buddy? You heard of the television network NBC, buddy?" He proceeded to question me in a patronizing, schoolteacher tone.

"Yes, it certainly rings a bell...buddy," the words leaving my mouth unsure of the offer about to be sold to me, or the name of the idiot selling it.

"They're shooting a reconstruction, buddy, on a new show called *The Other Side*, and chief...*you're* going to be reconstructed."

I had absolutely *no* idea what he was talking about. As he obviously loved to babble, I allowed him to proceed with the velocity he so blatantly adored.

From the burst of information he spewed, I gleaned the outline of the plot I was to color in order to earn my union right of passage. I was to play a male on this particular dramatic outing, thank God. (Already a HUGE step forward from previous roles.) I had been selected for this acting role due to my good fortune and, more importantly, my uncanny resemblance to a dead boy. The boy had obviously not shared in my fortunate streak. The possibilities awakened a morbid fascination within me, so with minimal details I agreed to take part in the shenanigans.

I drove to the location of the shoot in the remote mountains near Los Angeles, the air crisp and cold in the closing hours of the remaining day. As my car wound slowly and intentionally up the circumference of the hillside, I hoped that this climbing path would become a metaphor for my steadily climbing career. As I pulled into the location, people scurried around me, industrious with their specific tasks, a hundred bodies—each representing a piece of the elaborate puzzle.

The side of the mountain was illuminated by harsh, huge film lights strategically placed as if the corner we happened to be filming on had escaped the onslaught of night. I stood there, my elongated shadow stretching back behind me, staring out into the blackness.

In the far corner of the hustle and bustle stood two gaunt figures. A weathered, unkempt man, his hair wispy and white, and a tall woman, plump from the fruits of life, dressed in expensive yet ragged clothes. They clutched each other in their inappropriate attire entangled as one, trying to gain some comfort from the night's harsh elements. The two were very much removed from the goings-on around them. Their piercing eyes followed my every movement as I meandered from the comfort of my car into the frigid night.

I was methodically paraded from figure to figure on the set and introduced to my night's coworkers. I awaited my formal introduction to the strange couple, but it never came. My presence skirted skillfully around them. They were fussed over at regular intervals, which gave them an uneasy sense of importance, leaving me ever more curious as to their identity and purpose.

I approached the director, my interest now piqued as to who they were. He paused, placing his hand slowly on my shoulder. His eyes flitted across every inch of my face, not uttering a single word. He began to sigh with weighty breath, his pupils now locked onto mine. The air from his lungs almost completely expelled before he uttered his first syllables.

"You should come and meet the boy's parents. They wanted to see how it happened. Get some closure. That's okay, right?" He asked, not really looking for permission from me, more so instructing me as to how this bizarre proposition should make me feel. A huge burden was placed clumsily around my neck. I had absolutely no idea what to say to these distraught people. The joy and excitement of the prospect of performing in front of a camera was sucked from my veins with each heavy breath of the grieving parents.

The boy's story was told to me as follows: For weeks he had been troubled nightly by dreams of sprinting in a race he would never win, no matter the effort he put forth. He awoke unrested and confused from his nightly races. He told his parents and friends of the strange and intense recurring dream, looking for a simple answer so he could return to the seemingly idyllic life he had become accustomed to. As the weeks progressed the dreams became more vivid to a point where he would awake to find his feet bleeding, dirty, and bruised. This left the boy frightened and ever more perplexed as to what was happening to him in the midnight hours. He knew the events taking place were an illusion, yet the experience was leaving the harsh scars of reality. He had never once contemplated any aspirations of being an athlete in his daily life, but his subconscious had other definite plans for him that now it was methodically putting into place.

Ultimately, the boy met his untimely death on a cold night much like the one upon me now. In the early hours of the morning, an eighteen-wheeler rounded the corner of a mountain pass on its downward descent. Its headlights cut into the night air, where the figure of the boy was suddenly illuminated. The teenager was sprinting along the central divider of the cold tarmac road, wearing only his underpants and nothing more. The young man's eyes were firmly closed as he slammed headfirst into the truck, the impact killing him instantly. The boy's death was deemed a very rare case of sleep running. One of the only documented occurrences known, and a story I would now have to bring to life.

I was absolutely horrified listening to the story. My mind was racing…wait a minute! Bloody hell, my wardrobe would once again be a little scarce, obviously. I wasn't even sure if I was wearing underpants tonight. What if they weren't going to supply some for the shot? This could turn into a streaking catastrophe. It would end up like a *Benny Hill* escapade rather than a fitting tribute to the boy. I wonder where the craft service table was—I had a sudden desire for red licorice. NO NO NO. Stay focused, one train of thought, say something meaningful to the boy's parents.

"I'm so sorry…Would you like something from craft service?" I mumbled.

Perfect. A true master of linguistics. With a God-given knack for comforting words. Was it really that stupid a comment to make to the boy's parents, though? After all, the craft service table always gave me great comfort…actually I would like to withdraw that comment. Comfort was the wrong word—constipation or diarrhea were probably better descriptions—which in turn would mean that yes, my outburst was totally ridiculous, come to think of it.

When shooting a film or television show that requires some sort of nudity, I came to discover that these scenes are always shot first on a production. The bigger the star, the more relevant the rule. Hollywood has been burnt one too many times in the past. Actors would shoot half a film, with millions sunk into the project, only then to turn around and tell the director they see the naked scenes differently. This difference was usually that they saw their character clothed. With too much invested, recasting is not a viable option, so the actor takes the helm and steers the direction of the often pivotal scenes. Giving up control on a project to an actor isn't really at the top of the movie studio's list of priorities. So the naked bits go first, and if they don't go, the actor soon gets recast with a more accommodating body.

For my particular reenactment the Hollywood rules remained the same. The palm of my hand was still warm from my introductions to everybody as my near-naked, freezing body sprinted up and down the stretch of wet road.

Obviously, the director could not have me run headfirst into a barreling big-rig. I did have my standards, though you would never have guessed it from my slew of projects thus far. Death by acting was definitely not something I aspired to. To get around this minor problem, the moment of impact was filmed backward. My head was placed against the cold, metallic grill of the stationary truck. With the word "ACTION!" echoing through the peaceful mountainside, the truck began a high-velocity reverse maneuver. And so began my naked sprint—backward. Take after take. Eyes closed, underpants on, nipples freezing off. Later to be reversed in the editing room with full impact. Quite literally.

The strangeness of the evening has to this day never left me. A group of adults collected together for one main objective: to get the best possible shot of me running half-naked, backward and in my Y-fronts, in the middle of a desolate hillside road. I have often heard of people having nightmares, of going to work and entering an important meeting to find they have no clothes on, awakening harshly from the scene to discover it was nothing but a strange dream. This for me now was a twist on that classic nightmare. I had actually shown up to work, and I was the only one not fully clothed, but I was *performing* a dream and not actually having one. It was all very strange indeed.

More than anything, though, what stays with me is the image of the boy's grieving parents. By the end of the evening I still had absolutely no idea how to deal with the situation, so I myself just slipped back into the night. Unwilling and unknowing as to what to say to them or how to say good-bye, knowing it was actually their son they wanted to say good-bye to. I couldn't help associating this whole sad situation with the film *Running on Empty*. The film's pivotal scene was playing over and over in my mind for the entire evening, in which the parents of the main character have to make a tough choice. They choose to cut all ties with their teenage son so he has the opportunity to create his own life. These parents, regrettably, never had any kind of choice; their ties with their teenage son were cut by a random act. They stood there that night obviously wishing they could shoot some moments of their own lives in reverse as I had the truck scene, regaining some of their past joy. *Running on Empty* seemed very fitting for their own ghostly demeanor, trying to gather together the remnants of their lives having faced a parent's worst nightmare: the burial of a child.

I drove to the foot of the mountain in silence and headed back into Hollywood, returning to the body of my own life as the sun arose on another day full of possibilities and ways to earn a living to keep me in this strange place. Now I just needed to convince the government to let me stay a little while longer. For me, although fast becoming an illegal immigrant, the sun now shone just that little bit brighter and with more hope, beginning my new day a full-fledged member of SAG, my rite of passage now earned…

…streaking.

CHAPTER SEVENTEEN

੨**

GREEN CARD, 1990

Directed by Peter Weir.
Brontë (Andie McDowell), a New York horticulturist, finds the perfect
apartment with a greenhouse in the heart of the city. Unfortunately for
her, it is in a "married couples only" building. Georges (Gérard
Depardieu), a French immigrant, is desperately in need of a green card
to allow him to stay and continue working in the United States. The two
soon find each other and enter into a marriage of convenience with
mutual benefits. The unlikely pair finds themselves now coping with
life—together. Nominated for an Academy Award for Best
Original Screenplay.

Life imitates art. Enough said.

CHAPTER EIGHTEEN

HONEYMOON IN VEGAS, 1992

Directed by Andrew Bergman.
On her deathbed, a mother makes her son promise to never get married. This scars him psychologically and ultimately blocks his commitment to his girlfriend. The thin plot involves one bride (Sarah Jessica Parker), one groom (Nicholas Cage), and thirty-four flying Elvises. The comedy is inevitably set against the neon backdrop of Las Vegas.

After two years the honeymoon period that never was had come to an abrupt end. Luckily, the green card wouldn't expire for quite a few years more. So, I was legally free to work as I pleased.

An old joke in Hollywood about actors goes something like this: A well-trained, talented, and handsome *working* actor walks into an agent's office and says: "I would like you to represent me. I have experience, talent, and enthusiasm."

The agent carefully looks the actor up and down and says, "A *working* actor, eh? Actually, you do look very familiar—which restaurant do you work at?"

As an actor arriving in Hollywood, you imagine the streets will be paved with gold. Regrettably, this is not the case. Not only are the streets not paved with gold, it is more than likely that you are literally going to have to take a job paving them yourself just to pay the bills.

Most actors in fact find themselves not actors but waiters. They slave for a pittance in restaurants, serving the upper echelon of the Hollywood elite as they dine over deals. This type of utterly crap work has been appointed to the very prestigious category of the "food service industry." The sole purpose of this categorization is to make the sad saps working in the field feel slightly better about themselves. Having said that, the work does have its benefits. It provides a flexible schedule, a job requirement prized by aspiring actors, allowing them the opportunity (if they are lucky enough) to occasionally audition. Surprisingly, you find out that very few people actually do audition on a regular basis.

Many people living in Hollywood just like to introduce themselves as an actor. You will run into them on every boulevard and corner of the city. The title "actor" certainly carries with it some mystique when citing it to someone as your profession. In reality, if the "food service professionals" were truly honest with themselves, acting is a lifelong ambition that they don't have time to aspire to anymore—due to their waiter commitments.

For me, working in a restaurant was never an option. Aside from my multiple and varied food allergies, I had developed a lack of patience for obnoxious, wealthy, eating-at-fancy-restaurants bods. Instead of joining the silverware armed forces, my particular talents were directed toward a far more devious and artistic form.

I soon discovered I had acquired a natural, God-given talent in the ever-expanding field of computer forgery. It was not really the sort of legitimate job you could as an aspiring graphic designer go away to study, though I actually did study it somewhat under the guise of a degree in advertising and graphic design. Most certainly, however, the best lessons in forgery were self-taught through daily necessities. That is, if the right devious streak lay within you. In my case, it most certainly did. I had seen the benefits of my deceptive talents previously. Memories of my forgery apprenticeship in England, when I had manifested the Warner Bros. labels and identification badges for my little run-in with Joe Macher, now seemed amateurish in comparison to the new canon of my work. I had soon refined my craft and reached a level of excellence where even the appropriate authorities could not decipher my handiwork from the real McCoy.

I realize, of course, that after revealing my talent it is probably best not to go into too much detail above and beyond what I've already divulged. That being said, and now being as vague as possible, I will narrate as best I can the following tidbit:

Movie stars, as presented to us by the media conglomerates representing them, really are a part of the huge facade that is Hollywood. Nobody can look *that* perfect all the time, and believe me, nobody ever really does. I spent many countless days when auditions were few and far between being honestly employed in another field courtesy of the film studios. *Hollywood's digital beautification service industry,* or more commonly known as *computer retouching.*

I was paid ridiculous amounts of money for my specialist skill. This entailed digitally touching-up the Hollywood elite known to us all as movie stars, thus perpetuating the public's desire for human perfection. The raw, and I do mean absolutely *raw*, photographic shots of Hollywood's top players would be delivered to me for routine refining. Subsequently, they would each leave my computer screen with sparkly white and straight teeth. Bags and lines would be removed from around their eyes at the touch of a button. Signs of nights spent boozing were erased, and, naturally, inches were taken from their newly sculpted calves and bums. Heaven forbid the public should ever see them as real, flawed people.

For most people in the entertainment graphics industry this was considered a fantastic job. For me, though, it only provided a good paycheck and, most devastatingly of all, countless mind-numbing hours of frustration. I helped establish numerous stars with beautiful public images rather than using that time to sculpt and shape my own image and propel it to the forefront of the scene. This frustration resulted in my working only when I really needed to, so as not to completely destroy my own soul.

When you reach the pinnacle of a legitimate, profitable job in Hollywood, you can be sure it won't be long before the darker underbelly of the field also pays you an unannounced visit. For me, that inevitable call came at the end of a long, sweltering summer day. The phone startled the humid air without a care for its heavy tranquility. At the other end of the receiver spoke somebody who identified himself to me as "Larry with a Y," from a less-than-reputable gossip tabloid magazine. He worked for the kind of supermarket fodder everybody says they totally despise, yet all secretly flip through when the slightest opportunity arises to confirm their disgust.

Larry proceeded to speak to me in a very direct, clean, sharp, and crisp manner, using only the words that were completely necessary to emphasize his point. No more, no less. I pictured some sort of fifties' private-investigator type on the other end of the phone with a square, cleft chin, wearing a trilby hat and chain-smoking to further deepen his gravelly voice. A fan was surely revolving slowly high above his head, light cascading in through its hypnotic, tired revolutions, illuminating the smoke.

"I have a retouching job for you. I was given your name. I trust it's alright that I call you directly. It's a rush job that I will need first thing tomorrow. Your generous pay, of course, will reflect the quick turnaround—"

He paused abruptly as though still in mid-sentence, waiting

for my response, as if his allotted time with me had run out. It was as if he did not want to waste any more of his or my precious time if I was any kind of respectable, upstanding citizen. Luckily for him I had the ability to be less than upstanding, and on this occasion I was completely intrigued by his declamation.

I fired back with, "What kind of job is it and how much dough are we talking here, Larry?"

There you go, good boy—cut to the chase. No faffing around. I thought I would play the shifty geezer at his own game and keep my questions short and direct, putting on my poker face until he revealed his hand.

"It's a Nicolas Cage retouching job. A wedding picture of him and Lisa Marie Presley. Your compensation will be $5,000 cash for your night's work," he continued, speaking with absolutely no emphasis on a single word.

Is he having a fucking laugh? Five thousand dollars for a few hours' work? I paused for an instant, listening to the heavy sound of him drawing on his cigarette as I tried to justify the inevitable bout of dishonesty to my conscience. I was helping glamorize an obviously special day for Mr. Cage and his beautiful bride. Probably even doing them a favor, making sure they looked their best for the world to see, my good deed passing by totally unappreciated. Maybe I had not given the supermarket tabloids enough credit in the past. Maybe their dodgy reputation was itself a Hollywood facade. Maybe they were all just regular, misunderstood, church-going tabloid citizens. Of course I rapidly, consented to being a co-conspirator, and the images I was to retouch that evening were e-mailed directly to me. An e-mail address Larry with a Y strangely already possessed within his computer database.

The raw materials arrived promptly, popping up on my computer monitor within seconds. The deal was signed, sealed, and by the morning would hopefully be delivered to the notorious tabloid. Maybe I had been completely wrong with my assumption of tabloids…then again, maybe not. I was about to learn that the limited amount of faith I had in the humane aspect of tabloid magazines was obviously way too generous.

As I opened my e-mail with a fair amount of intrigue, the beautification of Mr. Cage and Ms. Presley took on a whole different spin. I stared at the image of their glorious private day. It was a photo of the pair walking down nature's own aisle on the island of Hawaii. But I could easily have been staring at a picture of the Muppets. This amazing *exclusive* wedding shot looked as though it had been photographed from England all the way to Hawaii, using some antiquated crap telephoto lens that was scratched and out of focus. The photographer's thumb was the only clear part of the shot, protruding crisply into the frame. Is Larry having a fucking laugh at me? Am I to be the provider of some giggles for him and his motley crew?

To be fair, you could tell (if you squinted really hard) that there were two shapes, or maybe if you stretched your imagination, possibly even human forms wearing dark and light clothing. Conceivably, one of them being a woman. Or maybe I was just projecting a female figure for the sake of Mr. Cage's heterosexual wedding vow credibility. The couple had arranged a very secluded ceremony, far from the lenses of the paparazzi and prying public scrutiny. Was I really going to taint their special romantic day with a fraudulent matrimonial picture? Don't be silly—for $5,000, of course I was. I needed to move quickly, time was ticking.

I worked feverishly through the night, trying not to dwell

on my nagging, debilitating conscience. I gathered as many Nicolas Cage and Lisa Marie Presley shots as I could from previous public events. I would at least have a truthful, yet corrupt, starting point for my work. A wedding dress was taken, or I should say "borrowed," from a picture of Slash's nuptials from *Guns and Roses* that I stumbled upon. His wedding had also taken place somewhere tropical, so the light and scenery nearly matched perfectly. I snatched a bouquet from another random wedding shot, Lisa Marie's head from a red-carpet event where she had been conveniently photographed in profile, and gradually built up the tropical skyline.

The only real problem I encountered was Nicolas Cage's noggin. I couldn't for the life of me track down a suitable image of him where he wasn't wearing sunglasses. I wouldn't dare have him look so casual in his wedding photograph. This was a serious event after all, not a dodgy movie premiere. What do I do? Did I have any conscience left? Well yes, but it was also nearly 4 a.m., fuck it—sunglasses it was.

The wedding photograph was finally composed and completed. Nicolas Cage and Lisa Marie Presley's images, to be fair, were certainly used in the making of it. That night, though, I single-handedly proved the saying *the camera never lies* to be an outright, bold-faced lie. I felt great about my handiwork and the effect of the final produced portrait, but I had sold my soul to the devils at the supermarket tabloids to produce it. How absolutely disgusting.

I attached the image to Larry with a Y's direct e-mail address (which he'd provided), hit the send key, and was fast asleep by 4:30 a.m. Having spent the night staring at Nicolas Cage and Elvis's daughter, I inevitably dreamed of the film *Honeymoon in Vegas* with the few hours of shut-eye I managed to achieve before morning. It was a hilarious comedic performance by Mr. Cage, without a doubt. Well, at least it was funny in my dream. The film turned out to be a bizarre foreshadowing of Mr. Cage's life, intertwining and twisting with his reality. Along with the thirty-four flying Elvises portrayed in the film, Cage himself would in the future fly into Hawaii to marry Elvis's daughter. Very strange. I awoke at 9 a.m. and tried to jolt myself awake with a bucket of coffee. I turned on the television to catch up on the news.

To my utter and complete horror, my night's work was displayed on every channel I flipped to. News channels, music stations—even fashion television. I couldn't get away from my lie. Specialist commentators were being brought in to critique Mrs. Cage's dress, bouquet, and general wedding grandeur. The ensuing discussions commented on the posture of Nicolas Cage and the location and the weather conditions, to which nobody was any the wiser.

The power of the media showed its true strength to me that morning. Something I had pieced together four and a half hours ago in my bedroom was now in millions of peoples' homes being force-fed to them for breakfast. Instantly. It was a discussion point. A pictorial, recorded fact presented to the unsuspecting public. Weeks' worth of fodder for the masses of trickle-down entertainment programming. I felt absolutely terrible. Whenever the design for the wedding dress was discussed, I felt as though the fraud squad would soon be kicking down my door, led by a furious, gun-toting Vera Wang and her fellow posse of outlaw designers.

I had also betrayed a fellow thespian. How could I make myself feel slightly less disgusting and bolster what little was left of my soul? Well, a check for $5,000 from Larry with a Y

140

would certainly help ease the pain. It was a definite starting point.

When you deal with unscrupulous people, becoming one yourself, expect to be shafted. It's a fact. It goes with the territory, and I was in for a royal shafting. The only method I had of contacting good old "Larry with a Y," I soon discovered, was his e-mail address. His cunning manipulation of our conversation was now apparent. I felt genuinely at the time that he had provided me with all the relevant information I needed. Hindsight, though, had just left me with doubts. Very thin ice to be walking on with such a man. The transaction had all happened so quickly, Larry's full name, address, and phone number just seemed irrelevant at the time. An afterthought. Nothing could be more relevant to me now, though. I e-mailed Larry and I waited for his response.

Nothing.

I e-mailed him again trying a different tactic, congratulating him on the extensive coverage the picture had received.

Nothing.

Maybe Larry was just busy with deals on the purchase of the picture. I e-mailed him again the following day, only this time my address had been blocked by the recipient. I use the word *recipient* because I called the notorious tabloid where Larry supposedly worked. "Larry with a Y" was instead Larry with a big F U. He didn't work there. Nobody called Larry had ever worked there as far as they knew. They had no knowledge of the man, the picture, or what I was talking about.

I'm sure somebody got very wealthy from the picture I digitally created. It ended up being splashed on practically every periodical and news station around the globe. It just certainly wasn't Mr. and Mrs. Cage or myself. Pursuing the case and its ramifications was absolutely pointless.

At this juncture I would like to apologize to Nicolas Cage and Lisa Marie Presley; it was a terrible thing to do. Especially the whole wedding vow sunglasses debacle I initiated. Hindsight also has a tendency to scold you at a very audible decibel. Some people would call my financial loss and total shafting instant karma in its most pure form. I prefer to use the less spiritual term…

A total fuckup on my part. Plain and simple.

CHAPTER NINETEEN

§

LAP DANCING, 1994

Directed by Mike Sedan.
Angie (Lorissa McComas) is an aspiring actress trying to make it in Hollywood. A screen test for a film requires her to be naked on camera, something she's uncomfortable with. To overcome her fear she works at a strip club so she can learn to be at ease with her clothes off. Released to coincide with Showgirls, the film is pumped full of actresses so surgically enhanced that their chests resemble hot air balloons.

"Can you work today?" pleaded the desperate voice on the other end of the receiver. Pages of a book frantically sounded as they were turned, roughly thrown against one another. The sound of muffled voices asking the same question to countless other actors echoed in the background as if I were in a strange dream.

Without waiting for a reply, my agent continued hastily. "You have one hour to get ready and be on set. The director absolutely loved your picture. Oh, and bring a tuxedo jacket and a bow tie with you."

In a situation such as this there is very little need for excessive banter. Asking if I was interested or even available for work would just be a formality. They needed me desperately for a job, and I needed a job desperately. I was looking now for an honest day's employment away from counterfeiting, so their proposition was a match made in exploitative film heaven. I, of course, needed the money to pay my rent so I could stay in the city and struggle some more. I was also getting the chance to take my Oscar party tuxedo on its sixth outing. Did I really need to question the fantastic offer? The agency certainly owed me a respectable day's work by now; how bad could it possibly be?

143

With a crumpled Los Angeles city map in hand, I aimed toward the general vicinity of the set. Whenever I traveled in Hollywood I inevitably got lost on its intersecting numerical motorway system, literally a world away from the roadways I was used to in England. I soon came to accept this vehicular confusion as the norm when driving in Los Angeles, always adding more time accordingly. To add to the duress of having to figure out the road system, my mind would at some point take control of the wheel, altering my intended destination drastically. Then came that annoying little voice in my head: "You're going the wrong way. You're going THE WRONG WAY. You see that turn back there? That was your exit. You just passed it and there's not another one for miles." And this all in a condescending "I told you so" tone. On this rare occasion, though, I made it to the film set without a solitary mistake. This bizarre occurrence only served to assure me that some sort of divine intervention was at work. I was meant to be in this film, destiny had beckoned forth my weary, confused car.

I walked onto the dusty, bustling soundstage and proceeded to perform my now-familiar on-set routine. I checked in with the various Neanderthals clutching their prized walkie-talkies (they *are* a sign of importance, after all) and set about my task to uncover the film's basic premise. What seemed like a common investigative scenario on this occasion would prove itself slightly less challenging, Sherlock Holmes would not have to be called upon today. It was no great feat to unmask this obviously very intellectual—well, at the very least *stimulating* movie—even for the most basic of talkie-walkie primates.

Dressing room doors opened around me as if they were dominoes falling one by one, perfectly choreographed as if I

144

was in the middle of a Busby Berkeley film. The names Bunny and Amber echoed from one headpiece to the next, and a plethora of half-naked women proceeded to walk toward the set. The only things on the girls were the eyes of every man around them.

Like Stevie Wonder suddenly given back his sight, my vision instantly widened to reveal my surroundings, cunningly hidden from me by my very own retinas. This was not a film studio or even a real soundstage I was standing in. It was a dilapidated warehouse in the San Fernando Valley, an L.A. suburb on a shady industrial strip far from the public's curious eye. When the cry for wardrobe was heard from the depths of the set, a girl appeared with a handful of sparkly, primary-colored thongs. I made a grab for the script, flipping through the pages one by one trying to dispel my growing fear, but the papers offered me no solace. The text—large in size and small in quantity—left much to the financiers' imagination. Some serious fillers would obviously be taking place in the midst of filming!

I had arrived on the set of a porno.

When I hit puberty, I couldn't think of anything better than to be in a porno film as I pondered the adolescent life before me. Looking curiously through the pages of adult magazines left in Grange Park, I assumed this industry was just about mucking around with girls. I questioned if this job even really existed or if it was another schoolboy rainbow kiss myth dreamed up by Michael Nolan. Pornography is guaranteed to be a part of every schoolboy's dream job at some juncture in his life. Girls want to be doctors, ballet dancers, and mothers. Boys just want to be in porn or to play sports, or a bit of both if it can possibly be arranged, please, by a career guidance counselor.

The thing was—I was no schoolboy now—far from it. How could I justify working on this film in my own mind? Was I a serious actor or not? Rubber breasts and naked underpant runs had already made a complete mockery of my dignity. I had studied Shakespeare in one of the finest drama schools in London. I find it hard to believe Sir John Gielgud had suffered the same dilemma of the prospect of pornographic work (probably not, although you never know with that saucy minx). I couldn't possibly justify this to my family, or my acting teacher, and definitely not to my old grandmother waiting patiently in England to witness my debut on the telly. Would this really fulfill her desire to see me entertain and make her proud, sharing my accomplishments over a cuppa with the neighbors?

Fuck it.

I'll just do it for the boys back home. They could offer me the perfect perverted excuse, and would surely be the providers of some sort of twisted admiration.

The very thing that horrified me artistically about the film was the very same thing that kept me firmly there. Women with gigantic breasts. What is it about breasts that men find so fascinating? It's not like women have three noses; it's just two lumps of fat and muscle dangled from their chests. I can't help myself, though; I love everything about those portions of pleasure. I don't find myself staring at man-tits, however; it's purely a female thing—honest. I just don't feel the same way about Big Daddy's or Bernard Manning's upper body regions. I don't want to look at or even ponder their lumps, thank you very much. But a woman's chest I want to investigate, to prod and lift like a precarious experiment. I can think about them for days…if I'm really forced to, of course. Here before me lay

146

a strange opportunity, actually being paid to think about and interact with a plethora of breasts! My initial doubts bounced naughtily away. How absolutely delightful.

When literally situated in a room full of beautiful naked girls, all with amazingly firm, surgically enhanced assets, I was utterly disturbed by how quickly I became immune to it all. This wasn't at all how it was supposed to be! My fascination with their mammaries suddenly became talk of breast augmentation when I began working with them. I learned the stories behind each of the tiny scars adorning their in-progress bodies. As these Barbie-doll women pressed their glistening flesh against me during filming in a purely mechanical formula, the so-called sex objects became…human.

SAY IT ISN'T SO! Businesswomen, mothers, intelligent, manipulative, strong, fascinating, goal-driven women. NNNNNOOOOOOOOOOOOO! In the blink of an eye, I became the one more naked than them in my misconception and misinterpretation of the people I thought or hoped they might be.

The *Lap Dancing* girls were, in fact, a revelation to me, just not in the way I had initially envisioned. Every man around them was leering and fantasizing about them. They would approach the women stealthfully, clinging to their every word like hungry, blood-sucking, pornographic leeches. I, on the other hand, found myself talking to these naked women about business investments and children as they writhed above me. We spoke of their husbands, boyfriends, and football—things they were interested in. The tediousness and the total ridiculousness of the movie was soon put into perspective. It was actually only the real misinformed bimbos like myself that were making so little money on the film; the pornstars were all making a tidy sum. It was an easy financial justification for their role in the tomfoolery. Mine, of course, was a lot harder to explain. "I show my body. That's my business. I am, when you think about it, the walking definition of the phrase show business," and nothing seemed more logical coming directly from Amber's mouth to my ears at 3 a.m.

The more I developed a respectful relationship with these girls, the more comfortable they all soon became with me. The Neanderthals totally confused by the girls' ability to string a sentence together found themselves desperately circling us for a segment of conversation to latch onto, much to the director's amusement. He, in turn, presented me with more and more dialogue, latching onto the ladies' ease with me. I now had more scenes (fully clothed, thankfully) with multiple partners until I had elevated myself to be a key part of the film. If being an integral part of a soft-porn flick was an ambition... I had far outshone my goal. The days and nights soon folded into one another, along with my expanding role in the production.

Let's step outside the fishbowl and put things into perspective for a minute here. Maybe I had been whacked around the head by a 34DD breast one too many times at this juncture. Did I even want to be integral in the film, or did I want to gain back some of my lost integrity? With the beauty of hindsight, how would I now classify this film, along with my involvement in it? Not really a hard-core porn, but there was definitely nothing soft in the room either. A thriller, maybe? Thrills were certainly to be had if you viewed it, but definitely more erotic than thrilling. *Lap Dancing* most certainly wasn't a love story in the sense of what I had watched religiously growing up as a child. Love stories were films like *Casablanca* (the forbidden love), *Citizen Kane* (the love of a sled), or *Star*

Wars (a lonely farm boy and the love of a dirty old man that wanted to teach him about his saber). Well, then again, maybe in its own weird way *Lap Dancing* was just another different take on love, just in its most primal of forms. It was certainly as screwed up and torturous as most other love stories captured on film. Except with a much smaller budget and much bigger breasts.

What I uncovered at a later date was that the film was actually being marketed to the public as an *erotic romantic thriller*. Obviously, the film's makers and marketers themselves struggled in deciding which category the film should fall into, so they just chose three to cover all the options. But the word *romantic* squeezed into the title of the genre, that was even a shock to me. It just seemed a little...deceptive. Romance movies screw with people enough already when they are at their weakest. Could *Lap Dancing* be added into people's already played-with psyches? Could the Blockbuster corporation be so cruel?

To be fair, this soft porn film wasn't a total waste of my time and energy, although it certainly felt that way driving home at the end of the shoot. Looking back, this entire experience wasn't below me as I had initially thought when stepping in front of the camera. These girls weren't to be looked down upon for their choice in life or, to the other extreme, revered as untouchable icons or statues by the Neanderthals. They were real, flawed people just like me, struggling to survive in Hollywood, chasing their own version of the illusive dream. They were just a member of someone's family trying to make a living, gather their rent, pay their mortgage, and feed their children. Was it the stigma of society that had made me feel strange about this type of film? Or was I not as liberal as I had hoped? Am I really too good to work on an erotic romantic thriller?

This experience, above all else, really made me introspective about the time I had spent thus far in Hollywood. I had become average, really, in many aspects: a safe player, somewhat lethargic in the rays of the sun waiting for a huge film to come and discover me. I'm not Mr. Clever Clogs, but definitely not the silliest bloke in America. How had this transformation happened to me? I wasn't opposed to trying new things—was I? To being open to different experiences? It's just that at my age I already knew what I liked. I preferred to watch *Some Like It Hot* or *Singin' in the Rain* over Shakespeare. I preferred films in English in general to stuffy foreign films, although I'm not opposed to reading one—occasionally. I even have a huge list of subtitled favorites, come to think of it: *Betty Blue*, *Cinema Paradiso*…and many more, I'm sure, that I can't quite remember. So why, then, did watching a foreign film make me feel more educated and watching, or participating in, a soft porn make me want to shower?

When you reach a certain age, you become aware of a specific type of person. Middle-aged bods not living up to expectation. Men and women playing it safe, inevitably using their outdoor voices in indoor places. They have a primal call, laughing loudly, and in general drawing attention to themselves trying unsuccessfully to prove that their lives are not on a downward spiral and REALLY, they are enjoying their created reality. I didn't want to become one of those people. The *Lap Dancing* girls had not fallen into that trap. Society was not steering their ship. They seemed quietly secure in their own life's role and were willing to take a risk no matter what

150

anyone thought of them. There was, in fact, nothing at all safe about these adult actresses, and that was totally refreshing to me.

I needed to be bold in my choices with the knowledge that mighty forces would come to my aid if I just took a chance. I couldn't carry with me the fear of failure, which I had unknowingly begun to collect with rejections from numerous auditions. I deserved roles in amazing films, to work with incredible directors, and to truly be everything I had imagined growing up. My time on the porno had in the end taught me you can step into the ring with just about anyone from any walk of life and learn something. I was not trying to prove anything to society, I was trying only to impress myself now. I didn't want to represent safeness or untapped potential; that was the only role I couldn't accept.

Quite a day, really. An epiphany while working on a porno. Who would have imagined it? A morning that started out shitty and ended...well, to be honest, slightly less shitty. I now had under my belt my first speaking role in a Hollywood movie. Who cared if it was in soft porn or in an *Erotic Romantic Thriller*? But that wasn't all. As an added bonus, to put the proverbial cherry on top as I later discovered (in the "Romance" section of my local Blockbuster), they had placed my picture prominently on the DVD package so the world could see the fruits of my pornographic labors. I couldn't believe that the film's distributors were ruthlessly trying to destroy my epiphany with this embarrassment tactic! I needed to remember the words of encouragement from Amber and Bunny: I had to stay positive. I knew I could never hide from the experience now. I was thrown into the public forum in a film that anyone at anytime could go and pick up. It was a start to my Hollywood career. Be bold…Be bold.

ENJOY, GRANDMA!

Oh God. How embarrassing.

CHAPTER TWENTY

৯৯

TAXI DRIVER, 1976

Directed by Martin Scorsese.
Loner Vietnam vet Travis Bickle (Robert De Niro) drives his New York
cab on the night shift, observing the lowlifes who comprise most of his
fares. Wanting to connect with the people around him, including
campaign worker Betsy (Cybill Shepherd) and teenage prostitute Iris
(Jodie Foster), he hatches a plan to save Iris and clean up the streets.
His attempts are thwarted and his rage grows, turning him into a
walking time bomb in an urban nightmare.

It seemed like it would be an average audition on an average smoggy summer morning in Los Angeles as I pulled myself from the comfort of my bed. But it wasn't. In fact, it was far from average. The day would soon evolve into something that would alter my life and create an association far beyond anything I could have possibly ever imagined. The actual audition process seemed strangely effortless. It consisted of a *Titanic* sinking scenario that was improvised with a casting director, one of Hollywood's finest: Mali Finn. A woman who concealed her many years in the business with the deceptive, youthful sparkle in her eye. I was informed upon arrival that there were no actual specific roles yet. James Cameron would apparently be choosing the vessel's crew based on a combination of two factors: acting ability and period looks. Chance was left as the all important, omnipotent third factor.

The walls of the casting director's office were littered with tiny authentic crew and passenger photographs, as she painstakingly tried to cast actors as closely as she could to resemble their historical counterparts. So marked the starting point of a series of surreal experiences for me. I found myself in a vacant office, acting out the sinking of the *Titanic* for an audience of tiny sepia paper eyes. Miniscule photographic pupils that had actually witnessed the disaster firsthand. Most, of course, perished in the event I was to re-create nearly a century later so nonchalantly in front of them.

My audition was documented on tape and mailed off to James Cameron, who was already on location shooting the modern segment of his epic labor of love near Nova Scotia. Surprisingly, word was received quickly. Within a week I was at the director's bustling California office picking up a copy of the full script. It was here I caught a glimpse of my tiny piece of the enormous puzzle. I was informed that I would be playing the youngest steward on board the *Titanic* and would be acting opposite an Oscar-winning actress for most of my scenes. I was also informed that I would need a series of vaccinations and medical examinations in order to travel to the shooting location in Mexico, information that proved to be a little less exciting. Days later, a black stretch limousine was waiting patiently outside my house to whisk me away to the production, a spectacle which was already proving to be endless gossip fodder for the many tabloids.

I had waited so long to be a *real* actor and now lay before me a golden opportunity, a scenario that had played over in my mind a thousand times while growing up in London. A limousine and its pristine driver patiently waiting for my arrival downstairs, a man whose sole purpose was to be at my beck and call. I had to do everything I could to fully capture this moment, etching it deep into my memory and thus prolonging the driver's wait as long as I could without totally pissing him off. He stood guard outside my flat in plain, clear view of all the neighbors' twitching curtains, while inside I pretended to

154

gather my belongings in a carefree fashion (as if this kind of thing happened to me on a daily basis), passing backward and forward without haste in front of my open window. The fact of the matter was I had hurriedly packed two days before; my case was waiting patiently by the door the whole time. What was fifteen more minutes to the waiting driver, though? I glimpsed out one last time into the Los Angeles afternoon heat and the people focused on my waiting car from the confines of the unexceptional world around me.

I could hardly contain my excitement from the enveloping leather seats of the stretch mobile monstrosity, a true symbol of the Hollywood excessiveness that I, of course, adored. This kind of automobile wasn't really seen swarming daily in the rainy streets where I grew up, after all. A few hours into the journey we crossed the border from San Diego into Mexico. I racked my brain for as many random people to call as I could from the complimentary phone in the car. It just had to be done, as wanky as it might be. As I looked up, momentarily distracted from dialing a number, it was as though time had suddenly propelled me far into another world.

It was difficult to believe that the wealth of the American nation was propped up along its border by such poor, needy people. We drove past row upon row of shantytowns. Wooden shacks that these citizens called home, twisted and tumbling as if it was a city made of precariously placed cards under the blistering sun. Doors to their homes were left ajar as if there was nothing worth stealing, filled only with the dignity of their inhabitants.

I pressed my face to the car window, wide-eyed and totally shocked by what lay before me. I made as much eye contact as I could with the locals I drove past, but of they saw nothing, of course, but excess behind tinted glass. Children lined the roadside as my huge car traveled on, kicking up a steady stream of dust. Their youthful eyes vacantly stared for any sign of life from the limo's blacked-out rear windows. Each time the car stopped at a junction, a frenzy of tiny little hands would appear, tapping feverishly on the window and calling out to me desperately in their native tongue for any kind of help I could spare.

The joy, excitement, and arrogance I had felt upon leaving Los Angeles had been quickly replaced by an overwhelming sense of guilt and sadness. It struck me as more than a little ironic that I was making my way to participate in a film surrounding the horrors of an unforgiving class system. Here, now, in front of my eyes, nearly one hundred years later, was the most blatant wealth and poverty line I had ever physically experienced. The rich and the poor divided by the American border patrol. The metal gates sealed shut, separating the classes again just as they were on that devastating night aboard *Titanic*.

For the duration of filming I was to be housed in a five-star golf resort by the ocean shore, along with Leonardo DiCaprio and a plethora of thespians from Britain. The facilities were wasted on me, though. I had never even held a golf club in my hands before, and really had no desire to pick up the game now. It always struck me as a futile sport—wandering after a tiny ball you would strike randomly. The picturesque setting it was housed on was, all the same, quite breathtaking. Whales played in the ocean among the dancing rays of the sun clearly seen through my hotel bedroom window. Weathered fishermen could be witnessed at all hours wobbling on their bikes down the dirt road that marked the hotel boundary as they searched for the perfect spot from which to cast their lines. At the same time, the enormous, playful whales watched the attempts of the tiny, insignificant fishermen from afar.

As I was only scheduled to shoot a couple of scenes on the film, my estimated time on the movie would be about three to four days—at the very most—with travel and rest time. I knew I had to make every single second count. I sketched out a plan of visits to the set, even when I wasn't working, to soak up the magic that James Cameron would be surely weaving with his masterful precision. The very second I reached my destination I put my plan into action. Dumping my suitcase, I hurriedly jumped back into the limo and set out toward the film studio for what would be my first taste of the size and scope of the production.

The sun was setting in the Mexican town of Rosarito as we rounded a narrow corner. As if introducing his own offspring sprung forth from his loins, the driver proudly announced, "Señor, T-I-T-A-N-I-C," in an accent so thick it made the statement more of a guessing game than the proclamation he had intended. Far, far in the distance lay the outline of a ship dramatically backlit by the beauty of the rapidly darkening sky. Plumes of smoke, barely visible, were making their escape, weaving into the heavens from the ship's four funnels. I strained and squinted my eyes to decipher as much detail as I could, impatient at our slow and steady arrival. The famed ocean liner grew and grew in front of my eyes to the point where it filled my entire scope of vision. It was overwhelming in its grandeur and silent, dignified beauty. I stepped from the backseat of the car and walked toward the bow of the ship, unable to speak or take my eyes off it. I was completely unaware of everything and everyone around me.

It hadn't really registered until this point what kind of experience I was to be truly involved in. Women and children were being hoisted into lifeboats and dangled precariously over the depths of the murky water. I helplessly stood back and watched one of mankind's biggest catastrophes as it played out vividly before my own eyes. The magnificent replica ship constructed on a system of hydraulics slipped into the icy depths as James Cameron looked down from a crane placed high in the night sky. He floated above the action as if he were a religious icon barking out direction from the heavens to the scurrying passengers on the decks below. Absolutely stunning. And with the word "CUT!" excitedly projected from the director's bullhorn, the ship was eerily resurrected from its watery grave. The widespread panic dissipated from among the passengers as they prepared themselves to live the disaster again in front of the lens.

Without a doubt, everything on the film was on a massive scale, but as I looked closer at the minutia, I discovered that the extraordinary attention to detail was absolutely astounding. James Cameron had filled his movie with an attention to specifics like no other director I had ever heard of. The cutlery was made by the original *Titanic* supplier from Sheffield, England, each piece with the ship's insignia emblazoned onto the metallic surface. An emblem that no camera would ever pick up but undoubtedly layered each actor's performance. The carpets were woven to the specific ship's pattern by the original weavers. Stained glass doors were once again carved by original local craftsmen, and the tiny brass buttons on my steward's jacket each carried the Titanic White Star Line mark. Such detail immersed anyone who interacted with the props in the lavish world that was now lost forever. And so it went throughout the ship—detail upon detail replicated precisely with great love and care, duplicating history on film like never before.

My scheduled days soon turned into weeks on the film, weeks into months, and so on, while waiting for my moment in front of the lens. I was classed on *Titanic* under the very auspicious film term "Wet Weather Cover," a provision of film scheduling that basically means, when filming outside, if it begins pissing down with rain, they can at a moment's notice switch the schedule and shoot an alternate prepared scene that takes place indoors. One such alternate scene was my scene. Thus, every morning I would jump from my hotel bed, rip the curtains open, and breathe a huge sigh of relief as I felt the sun beating down upon my face from the clear blue skies above. I could have stayed in this Mexican beachfront paradise forever, and now it was beginning to look like my wish might come true.

As the months passed I adjusted to my new life—wanting to work and actually participate in the film I nightly watched being pieced together but also not wanting to go back to the doldrums of my life in Los Angeles. Most days I would have a driver take me into the central section of the fishing town to browse the shops. As the limousine arrived on an unusually windy Mexican day, the same daily bizarre pattern of events played out before me. Hoards of children would swarm the doors of the car, arms outstretched with the faint hope of receiving some money, tugging on my clothes as I stepped from the vehicle. The more inventive nippers would try to convince me that I needed to buy the entire massive box of bubble gum they struggled to carry with them. One could only hope that this wasn't their complete food source and financial centerpiece for the entire year.

159

The town, as a whole, naturally assumed I must have amazing quantities of money from the very fact that I would daily step out of a stretch limousine. The trips themselves, therefore, were absolutely pointless if you actually wanted to purchase something. If you suddenly had the overwhelming desire to buy a plastic donkey wearing a sombrero from any one of the shops, you could be sure the starting price in the haggling wars would be around the thousand-dollar mark. Spending time, therefore, would ultimately be the only usual daily transaction.

I wandered vacantly among the now-familiar winding, dusty streets on a day like all others until it hit me. Quite literally. A tiny drop of rain falling from a single cloud in the sky onto my sunburned cheek. As though it was a tear cascading down my face at my impending departure. SHIT! My time had come. I needed to get to the Twentieth Century Fox studio, and quickly.

I hailed the first taxi driver I could find. A shifty bugger that seemed as eager to move as a man condemned to stroll to the electric chair. I did my best to hurry him along as he stared up at the sky and masterfully stated the obvious, "Rain, señor," in a speech pattern in check with his general velocity. He shielded his grubby hand with the frayed cuff of his old denim shirt and proceeded to smear the now damp dirt into mud on his windshield, lessening his already diminished visibility.

"I'm actually in kind of a hurry, sir. I need to get to the film studios as fast as you can, please," I pronounced, trying to conceal my general state of panic. The rusty Volkswagen taxicab chugged and sputtered off down the street leaving me alone in my thoughts, confused, nervous, and excited about the now-very-real prospect that lay before me.

160

"Movie star, eh?" the cabbie broke the silence, bringing me back into his molasses reality.

"No…not quite," I murmured, trying not to sound overly confident.

"You like pussy, movie star?" His gruff voice didn't miss a beat. The the driver continued on, asking this rather intriguing question, as if this train of thought perfectly followed the vagina conversation we had never pursued.

"I can get you the best pussy, señor movie star," he spoke proudly—filling in the silence that accompanied me in the backseat. Perfect. I had found a Mexican pimp cab driver who seemed more interested in staring at me for facial reactions to his statements than he was in looking at the curvature of the road. I ascertained that conversation with this imbecile should be kept to a minimum. I fast became a mute, shaking my head in answer to his onslaught of questions, and proceeded to stare out the dirty window avoiding eye contact with his shifty pupils at all costs.

Because I was distracted by the torrent of mental inner dialogue, I paid little attention to the familiarity of the road. Until, of course, he pulled his taxi into a deserted driveway alongside of a dilapidated home.

"What are you doing?" I nervously responded, snapping out of my inner trance.

"You come see my wife, movie star," the driver firmly requested, now staring coldly into my eyes.

Was he having a fucking laugh? I really couldn't think of a worse idea. Cab boy was as mad as a badger, but the thought of the woman that fell for this nutter was an even scarier prospect. I pictured the mother from Hitchcock's *Psycho* rocking in her window, waiting to greet me if I stepped in or, worse still, was carried across the threshold. I hadn't a clue where I was and now had absolutely no means of getting to the *Titanic* studio. All in all I was totally buggered—and, quite possibly, could be physically buggered at any given moment.

"You don't understand; I need to get to the film studio," I said, speaking clearly and slowly at a very audible level to avoid added confusion.

"I understand," he replied rapidly, pausing in wait for my next redundant statement.

"Okay, you understand. Help *me* understand. What do you want so we can get back on the road to the studio?" I tried to sound like I wasn't about to bargain, as I had nothing to offer the mad man.

"You come meet my wife," he repeated as if it were the only English sentence he spoke, smiling inanely at the end of his ridiculous demand.

"I don't have time to meet your wife," the sound of my voice gradually rising with the palpitations of my heart.

"You come meet my wife" he barked again, the words his now-familiar response.

There quite obviously was to be no haggling with his preposterous request. I had one of two choices. I could make a run for it in the pissing rain with the hope of finding the studio or, at the very least, another sane human being at some point along the deserted, soaked road. Or I could meet his wife and just pray there was a living female waiting to greet me in his home. And that I would leave his abode at some near point in the future—alive, and with my bottom intact. Unbelievable!

"Five minutes, then we go to the studio," I stated strongly, trying to stay in control of the rapidly spiraling situation.

Fortunately for me there was a woman in his house who did

actually claim to be his wife. Unfortunately for me she was as mad as, if not madder than, cab boy. His wife proceeded to demand the contents of my wallet to help feed and clothe her kids before her husband would take me anywhere, let alone to the studio. I had sat around uneventfully for months in the blistering sun, and now on the very day I was to film I was being blatantly mugged by Señorita Bonnie and Señor Clyde. It was my own little disaster movie playing out before me before I performed in the other, slightly bigger, disaster film.

I did make it eventually to the *Titanic* studio. Dampened from the rain and from my spirits after the taxi driver dropped me within distant sight of the studio gates. My wallet and ego were considerably deflated by cab boy, but I was still ready for my moment of glory: to be captured on film for an eternity. I had lost $120 that afternoon, but the thieves had lost their dignity in the process. I'm still not sure who paid the higher price. One thing I did know, though; I certainly felt like the bigger, wetter, imbecile...

Señor movie star.

CHAPTER TWENTY-ONE

꒰ꔹ꒱

TITANIC, 1997

Directed by James Cameron.
Fictional, romantic tale of a wealthy society girl (Kate Winslet) and a
poor, struggling artist (Leonardo DiCaprio) who meet on the ill-fated
voyage of the infamous unsinkable ship the Titanic. Love blossoms as
disaster strikes in the film's monumental crescendo, penned by history
itself. Nominated for the most Oscars in Academy Award history, it
subsequently became the highest-grossing movie of all time.

It had been quite the day already, thanks to my harrowing journey with the Mexican version of Norman Bates. After all the excitement, I could do with a cuddle, as long as it wasn't from cab boy. Anyone else was fair game at this point. I crossed the threshold of the Fox Baja Studio knowing that the evening would be special, and it was. My sodden shoes walked across the gravel toward the all-encompassing ship that sat before me as if I were wandering on the sand to happen upon this beached behemoth. The ship consisted of a 775-foot-long, ten-story facade, with steam billowing from the funnels while it waited for the crew. At last I was here, ready to board.

Everyone said that making this film the way James Cameron envisioned it was an impossible task. The fact that by necessity the director also took on the entire construction of the Fox Baja Studio compound is almost inconceivable. The location would become the first built by a Hollywood major studio since the 1930s and became affectionally known as the "100 day studio," although it was probably called less lovely things by the workers who actually had to toil day and night to complete it. Cameron's dream occupied a forty-acre beachfront lot holding no less than the world's largest open-air tank, four indoor stages, dressing rooms, production offices, and a labyrinth of wardrobe, props, lighting, and set pieces. Who knew that it turned out to be cheaper to erect structures permanently from steel and to build dressing rooms rather than rent trailers? And so it was that we moved into our new lodgings with the stench of fresh paint permeating the interior of each building.

The Baja studio was ambitious. The film was ambitious. Drinking the local Mexican water was ambitious, if not ludicrous. In fact, daily safety briefings on set would end with, "Let's be careful and don't drink the water…even if you're drowning in it." Mexican water is unlikely to ever be bottled as a life-giving elixir. It's more likely to be bottled as a tuberculosis aperitif, so the constant warnings and reminders were a good point well made by the film's safety crew.

Walking onto the main soundstage for the first time was breathtaking. At one end of the massive stage, lights burned brightly while illuminating a scene being shot. Like a moth, I was drawn into the wonder of the mystical glow before me. In my peripheral vision lay the first-class dining hall, the corridors of the great ship, and various staterooms hiding in the darkness, waiting for their time in the spotlight. As I reached the focal point of the scene, crowds of people stood huddled around stacked monitors, watching the filming unfold. I weaseled my way through the dusty cables and bare wooden outer walls only to step in front of the now-infamous grand staircase of the ship. As with the rest of the ship's details, the ornate wall paneling on the grand staircase was not typical plaster painted to look like wood but it was, instead, real carved oak, and the ornate cherub on the stairs was not plastic but cast in bronze. My eyes flitted from detail to detail in awe, and suddenly Jack Dawson was perched halfway up the staircase, extending his hand to Rose DeWitt Bukater.

"So, you wanna go to a real party?" he asked her.

Let me take this in for a second. Great. I wonder where craft services is.

Close to the main entry gate (within the watchful sight of Cameron's offices) were the dressing rooms for the *Titanic* cast. Housed in a huge, rectangular building they were a surprisingly peaceful sanctuary away from the throngs of industrious masses outside. As you entered the structure, to the right were the dressing rooms for Kathy Bates, Bernard Hill, Frances Fisher and on the opposite far wall were those for Leonardo DiCaprio, Billy Zane, and Kate Winslet. The rest of the cast ran down either side, connecting the key players. In the center of the rectangular building were makeup, hair, wardrobe, and props. Because there were such long setups between shots, and because the crew would typically work all night long, the corridors of the building resembled those of a college dormitory. People flitted from room to room to help pass the time with a chin wag; laughter and stories of the previous night's filming filled the air.

In James Cameron's wisdom, he had placed a TV and a VCR in each dressing room along with every previous *Titanic* film or historical documentary for us to scrutinize and analyze. In some local worker's wisdom, he had decided one day to walk off with most of the brand-new TVs and VCRs, leaving us huddled in the one spared dressing room for entertainment.

A few months after having settled in to my strange routine of daily disappointment at not filming due to the weather, I began to see the set I had visited countless times before with fresh, excited eyes as a performer. I was ready to get involved,

166

but the weather had other plans for my destiny. With mixed emotions I joined the rest of the boys huddled around a small telly, flipping through the adult channels. I had officially joined the *Titanic* masses of *hurry up and wait*.

The film's producers had hired an etiquette coach, Lynne Hockney, who in our downtime was to mold us heathens into Ladies and Gentlemen worthy of stepping on board the great ship. It was no small task when you consider cast and crew some days reached up to twelve hundred people. It was easy to see that she had an uphill battle spending even two minutes in the dressing rooms with us, gentlemen kitted out in the finest Victorian clothing, all of us in turn acting like prepubescent schoolboys. The prospect of analyzing and scrutinizing X-rated channels was the only thing able to quiet some of England's finest thespians, every camera angle and scene commented upon as if writing *An Astute English Gentlemen's Guide to Filth*.

The peanut gallery provided a constant running commentary to the already light-on-dialogue films they watched. "Blimey, the Bristol's on that one. Go on, my son, get stuck in! A little how's your father with that bird would go a long way. How do these geezers get these jobs? It looks like a badly packed kebab in there!"

Which roughly translates to, It's time for me to leave this bizarre group activity. I walked back to my dressing room, the testosterone swell following me down the corridor, and took off my woolen steward's costume, trying to keep my spirits up and my temperature down. So it wasn't my time to shine tonight. I was still on an epic scale film, and one day soon I was about to step in front of a camera opposite Academy-Award winning peers. I was here to prove that I was a legitimate actor worthy of Twentieth Century Fox's personal investment in me.

"EMMETT, YOU SHIFTY BUGGER!"

Oh no.

Excited footsteps chased the testosterone swell back to my dressing room. "Oi shifty, we just saw your big moment on the telly!"

The thought of *Lap Dancing* following me to Mexico hadn't even entered my mind, but like an exposed stowaway it was now uncovered for all to see. My *Erotic Romantic Thriller* had made an unannounced visit to the set and suddenly my moment of cinematic glory had all gone a little pear shaped. There was no escaping it. Remember Amber and Bunny? What would they do? They would try to put a positive spin on this trouncing.

Think quickly. I walked slowly back toward the boys, my own voice emanating from the the television speakers already pervading from the hallway. Think, think. I was an actor, so what if I was a storyteller in the genre of *Erotic Romantic Thrillers*. Being a storyteller of any description is a worthy way of spending one's life. It was still art, right? And art of any description is fundamentally important in the world. Okay, this was good... I was convincing myself. Keep going, shifty! In the ancient Greek court, the king would have a soldier, a philosopher, an astrologer, a doctor, and an actor. As actors, we are the world's storytellers and that, in itself, is worthy. *Erotic Romantic Thrilling* stories need to be told by someone; they needed to be told by *this* one. My stomach was sinking along with my concocted justification. Bollocks.

The flickering lights from the television flashed into the hallway and people were clambering up one another to get a view from outside into the already full-to-capacity room. My palms were sweating and my heavy footsteps seemed to echo with every slow, methodical step I took.

Divine intervention is a wonderful thing. It was at that point that the goddess, known by her human name as Frances Fisher, crossed paths with me in the hallway and extended an invitation to go into town and have a drink with her. Which, of course, I gladly accepted. For the time being I had circumvented my slaughter amid the thespians lying in wait and sharpening their tongues for my verbal career deconstruction.

Traveling to the simplest of locations in Mexico—even, for argument's sake, a restaurant—could still be a harrowing experience (as if I hadn't had enough trauma already). To put it nicely, corruption is something that seems to be taught in schools in Mexico. In fact, most men here are Olympic-caliber dodgy blokes. As our car traveled down the road into town, we would hit certain checkpoints guarded meticulously by police in full army fatigues. I wasn't ever sure what they were looking for, but they were not faffing about, that much I could ascertain. They entered our vehicle after stepping out from their shoddy sandbag huts, machine guns firmly gripped in their hands. They slowly scanned us from head to toe. For a boy who doesn't speak the language to be greeted by the barrel of a machine gun is never the most settling experience. Call me old-fashioned.

Of course, this was not the first time I had seen a gun. I had watched *Full Metal Jacket, Platoon, Top Gun, Scarface,* and Apollo Creed take a beating from Ivan Drago's guns countless times in *Rocky IV*. When the barrel of a gun is pointed directly at your head, it's as though all of time slows and your eyes focus intently on the cold, metal inanimate object. The silver flecks of chipped metal around the tip of the barrel were almost hypnotic, triggering a flurry of images as if my cerebrum was a This Is Your Life flick-book. (Please, mind, spare me the image of the bikini-and-rubber-breasts debacle.)

After a thorough inspection, Frances and I made it to the quaint beachfront hacienda and methodically plowed our way through a large pitcher of margaritas. It was a strange and disappointing night for sure, but what a wonderful way to waste my time. We drank and talked, our only interruptions being the deafening crack of thunder and then the sudden ringing of Frances Fisher's phone.

"Is Emmett with you, Frances? Change of weather, change of scene. We are going indoors to shoot the grand staircase now. We need you both back."

Would this day know no end to the dramatics? Was God having a giggle at my expense?

We jumped back into the waiting car, not even having the chance to digest my churning stomach full of margaritas mixed with a healthy shot of nerves.

It was time.

Quickly arriving back at the studio I was rushed through hair, makeup, and wardrobe placing my costume back on, with people fixing and pulling at me as I hastily made my way to set transportation. We were bundled into a minivan for the short ride from the dressing room to the set as if our driver was a Victorian mum taking her children to late-night-football practice. Kate Winslet, Kathy Bates, Victor Garber, Frances Fisher, and I packed into the van and did our best to avoid getting our costumes wet from the light sprinkle of rain. This all seems a little ironic now when looking back on and considering the scene we were about to film. We were escorted to the foot of *Titanic*'s grand staircase where James Cameron greeted us with his usual infectious enthusiasm.

The director was brilliant. An articulate, astute, fascinating genius; one of the most exceptional people I've ever met to this day. Cameron went into what was going on in my scenes both emotionally and logistically by giving me as much personal attention as he did the stars surrounding me. To throw an actor into a scene in a film doesn't take a genius. For a director to have mapped out logistically the position of every steward and key passenger on the boat at any given moment falls dangerously into *Rainman* territory. He literally knew which part of the ship my character had come from, how long it had taken me, the velocity I would have had to have been traveling, and he could dissect whose path I could have crossed and who I could have spoken to while ascertaining information on my travels. And here I was struggling to merely remember where the bathroom was that I visited every day. It was inspiring and intimidating in one fell swoop.

Cameron was a perfectionist and everyone knew he could do any job at any given moment on the set as well as if not better than any of us he had employed. For every actor and actress on the production, filming was a unique and arduous experience. This was the type of film on an epic scale witnessed by not even the most seasoned of thespians. It was as if this common bond united us in a long battle together and we were all comrades trying to make it through alive.

Kate Winslet had the hardest journey, but to her credit she never complained once about the conditions she was thrown into on a nightly basis. As the ship was being flooded the men could wear wet suits under their costumes to keep them warm.

Kate was dressed in the most delicate of chiffon costumes that flowed and became translucent when dipped into water, so a wet suit was not an option for her. She had to act in the early hours of the morning in dirty, freezing ocean water pumped into the ship, and her lips often became blue from the cold. She would then be thrown into a hot tub to raise her body temperature only to be thrown back into the freezing water, still never once complaining. Following Hollywood's golden naked rule, Kate Winslet and Leonardo DiCaprio's first scene together was in fact the shot in which Jack sketches Rose wearing only the Heart of the Ocean diamond while she is reclining on a chaise lounge. (Remember, naked shots of the actress or actor in a film always come first before they have a chance to back out.) The actors propelled into their first encounter with a natural yet uncomfortable excitement, elevating the underlying emotion of the scene. In the close-up shots of the sketching of Rose, James Cameron's hands can be seen drawing the masterpiece. That day Cameron also did the catering for the film, costumes, all the stunts, hair, makeup, security, transportation, and he made lovely cups of tea for everyone…probably.

My minutes on film had taken a night to shoot and now my time here in Mexico was all but over. The production was ready to ship me back, although I myself was desperate to keep this journey going.

I awoke the next morning forced into a last good-bye. I had heard stories of celebrities working on big budget films who wouldn't get out of bed for three-quarters of a million. I will always get out of bed for a cup of tea to do something I love. I'm happy living my life that way; it's healthy. I grabbed some of the hotel stationery and composed a letter to Cameron, a thank-you note mildly disguising my desperate plea to stay on board. I took a final limo ride to the set, the rain from the night before leaving the air fresh and alive. I walked toward his office and slipped the note under his door. I took one last look at *Titanic*, although half submerged in the murky water, seemingly calm and enjoying the blistering sun. Not a soul to be seen on its decks. I closed the door to my car and on this chapter of my life and headed back to the hotel to pack up my belongs. I waited in the lobby with my suitcase by my feet. The hotel concierge's phone rang and he signaled me over. A familiar voice on the other end spoke quickly and with authority. "Emmett, I know you were scheduled to leave tonight but Cameron wants you back on set, please."

And so my journey continued on, with Cameron placing me in a multitude of additional scenes over the following weeks. Maybe word had gotten back to him about my stellar performance in *Lap Dancing*? Of course, it had to eventually end, as all good things do. And as any good producer knows—and the veteran producer on *Titanic* was no exception—when a specific line item in a budget has been fulfilled, it needs to be checked off. Unfortunately, that line item was me. I even saw the dreaded final signal to Cameron. The producer simply ran his hand across his neck, mimicking it being cut like a scene from the *Godfather*, and Don Vito Corleone had sealed my fate.

One last tequila shot with the cast and then I finally climbed into my car, ready at last to be taken home. I slept in the car back to Los Angeles, and my driver made an unannounced stop at Cameron's Playa Del Rey special effects shop. I awoke, still drowsy from the journey, and followed the driver inside. Stepping into the warehouse was a surreal experience, as if an *Alice in Wonderland* moment had taken place. Had the shot of tequila really had a paper sign with the words "DRINK ME" beautifully printed on it in large letters? I had spent six months on board the ten-story, perfect replica of the *Titanic* and now before me was the same ship in perfect detail—only at one-twentieth scale. I was in comparison gargantuan, now unable to board the vessel before me ever again.

The next time I would talk to James Cameron would be at the *Titanic* premiere. This was a baby he had reared for years under harsh public scrutiny but was now ready to let the public have their judgment. In 1977, after seeing *Star Wars*, Cameron quit his job as a truck driver to enter the film industry. With *Titanic* he now would become the newly appointed king of the film world, the ruler of his own unique, watery galaxy surpassing his inspiration on multiple levels. I approached him at the after party extending my hand, still amazed from the film I had just witnessed as if I were conversing in a dream state. "I didn't think they made films like this anymore, James," I said. To which he paused, and with his usual dry delivery said, "They don't, Emmett."

With a wink of an eye the *Titanic* director turned and was swallowed up by a sea of people, disappearing once more into the cold December night.

CHAPTER TWENTY-TWO

な

2001: A SPACE ODYSSEY, 1968

Directed by Stanley Kubrick.
Mankind finds a mysterious monolith on the Moon. It is the year 2001,
and a technologically advanced human race, represented by the S.S.
Discovery and its crew—doctors Dave Bowman (Keir Dullea), Frank
Poole (Gary Lockwood), and their onboard, seemingly flawless computer,
HAL 9000 (Douglas Rain)—set out to discover the origins of the
artifact. The mission seems to be going smoothly until HAL malfunctions
and events spiral out of control.

In Kubrick's *2001*, man and computer turn from partners to enemies in a spectacular, trailblazing and philosophical masterpiece. Machines and technological advances were undoubtedly changing the face of cinema as the year 2000 dawned, but would this film really be a foreshadowing of the way things were to be? One could only hope not. As computer chips advanced at an ever-increasing pace, so was the business of filmmaking rapidly propelled forward. Inevitably, a new set of Hollywood moguls was born to rule the emerging digital frontier.

The Digital Entertainment Network, or DEN as it soon became known, was a cutting-edge company that owned the rights to a piece of futuristic Hollywood technology. The idea behind DEN was essentially to bring a catalogue of first-class entertainment on demand to your computer so you could watch your favorite programs when it was convenient for you, not when the schedulers wanted you to watch them. In essence, DEN provided was original, downloadable content, broadcast via the Internet to watch at the time of your choosing. It utilized the potential of your computer, with a full schedule of programs unavailable on regular television networks. With the click of a mouse you could catch up on your favorite shows, downloaded in an instant. Aimed at Generation Y, a new demographic largely untapped thus far, DEN set out to ride the wave of the dot-com explosion. It was "an entertainment company, exemplifying the pinnacle of a bright new dawn of computer monitors with Hollywood pizzazz." Or so the founders led everyone to believe at the slightest of opportunities, the words cascading from their lips like those of Baptist preachers to their faithful flock.

DEN's masterminds consisted of a trio of executives plucked from successful alternate careers. A step away from being used car salesmen, they were prone to the bad habit of cramming a plethora of buzzwords into the tiniest of sentences. Each man was bespectacled, frail, and pasty due to his obvious lack of exposure to daylight and fresh air. All three were also identically tailored, as though they shared one small wardrobe, adding to the confusion when attempting to distinguish among them. It was quite plausible to their whiz kid workforce that the threesome had nonchalantly discovered a way to clone themselves in their brief downtime. Each spoke with a fondness for non sequiturs as their voices overlapped like gentle, continuous ocean waves. They were inventors, but on a deeper level, believers torn straight from the pages of a classic science fiction novel.

Corporations such as Ford Motor Company, Pepsi, Blockbuster, NBC, Chase Capital Partners, Microsoft, Dell, Intel Corp., and the infamous Enron were all allegedly transfixed by DEN's possibilities, rapidly investing or pledging large sums of money on behalf of the promising new venture. Figures in the range of $70 million were offhandedly thrown about the walls of the offices as capital effortlessly gathered in order to launch the first phase of the new media company. The *Los Angeles Times* and *USA Today* battled, as usual, to one up each other, both leading with full-page stories about the seemingly glowing future of the burgeoning new media entertainment company. Stars were being courted and casts melded to interject into the lineup of the digital network's shows. All the while behind frosted glass doors the identical silhouettes of upper management plotted their slaughter of network television, each man trying his best to justify a multi-million dollar salary to his own conscience.

I entered the fold quite unaware of the project or technology I was about to step into. I auditioned at a converted Santa Monica warehouse, now the central intelligence hub, a stone's throw from the glistening Pacific Ocean. From behind their twinkling eyes, management was happy to enlighten me with the prospect of starring in "one of their most promising shows," the words escaping from their mouths only to be caught with ease by my burgeoning ego.

Dot-com decadence exuded from the white walls of the building in the form of high-priced, vibrant artwork and furnishings. State-of-the-art computer systems were stacked, reaching from polished concrete floor to vaulted ceiling. Twenty-somethings scurried industriously backward and forward to each other's monitors as if they were worker bees feverishly deciphering a money code. All the while the queen bees kept watch over the buzzing hive from the surrounding maze of offices.

To even gain entry to the back area of the office, a long legal document had to be perused and autographed. I'm quite sure I signed over my retinas that day somewhere in the fine print of the contract. As a safety precaution, tucked away in some hidden clause, I think they also received the cornea of my firstborn child, just in case I was to genetically pass on any top-secret information about their top-secret venture. I was auditioned to play a naughty devil from the depths of hell, cunningly disguised as an English schoolboy and thrust upon the American educational system. Strangely, this was a role I had played daily, for free, at Cypress Junior School some years before, and now lay the prospect of financial gain for my tomfoolery.

After stumbling through a page of clumsy dialogue, almost instantly I was informed that I was cast as the lead in *Redemption High*, in what was to be one of DEN's flagship shows. What was to follow all became a blur. Costumers ran intrusive tape along the length and breadth of my body, while in my hands were thrust more legal documents to sign and a script to consume before the day was through. If it was a shifty little devil they wanted me to play, it just meant dropping my daily facade to the world—how much easier could this job be?

Every indicator led me to believe this was what I had worked so hard for. I had finally deciphered the monolith known as Hollywood. I now clutched a contract stating quite clearly that I had a steady job on a series. The network had guaranteed a good amount of shows they were willing to shoot, thus helping to reinforce my stability. And, on top of it all, a regular acting paycheck was soon being dropped into my mailbox to be ripped open excitedly on a weekly basis. Things were good. In fact, putting all modesty aside, things were fucking fantastic.

Due to the network's relentless marketing efforts, they had managed to lure in some established celebrities to give each show some initial credibility. Actress Carrie Fisher was to come on board in a piece entitled *Denmother*. I use the words *Carrie Fisher* very loosely, of course. What I really mean is childhood fantasy **PRINCESS SEXY RETURN OF THE JEDI DOMINATRIX LEIA!** Director Randal Kleiser of *Grease* fame was to take the helm on another fantasy series. Rounding out the cast in my show was the actor Judge Reinhold, from the childhood classic *Beverly Hills Cop*, a film that undoubtedly proved to be a huge American travel instigator for me. To top it all off, my show had an Academy Award–nominated director behind the camera. It seemed as though some of my great cinematic influences had started to converge. There I was in the middle of the fray, still wide-eyed with wonder waiting now to stand next to the people I had watched from afar on screen for so long.

Redemption High, it became clear, would rely predominately on special effects creating a fiery devil's lair around us. It was here I encountered my first real introduction to green screen acting. The color green photographed in the background of a scene allows special effects wizards to place in any digital artificial backdrop they want, creating a very different effect. The end product can be quite spectacular. But while filming, this technological feat meant that explosions would be a crew member off-camera pathetically yelling "Bang." My interactions with the Dark Lord himself would be conversations with a tennis ball hung from the ceiling, representing the height of his head. Not really the most intimidating of presences but reaffirming my belief that John McEnroe was the devil after all, his precarious tightrope of anger now all too clear to me. Due to the excessive special effects, production costs for the show were said to have been

$100,000 for a mere six-minute segment. More disturbing to me was the fact that I found myself playing out cumbersome emotional scenes within an empty green void, as if I were acting in the depths of outer space. This adventure was more of a vacant space oddity than any kind of space odyssey.

Our production took over a studio located in North Hollywood. Sets were scattered from room to room in a dreamlike maze, throwing you precariously into a green, unfamiliar world. Ford Motor Company picked up the primary sponsorship of *Redemption High*, which meant I was soon presented with the keys to a brand-new, top-of-the-line Jaguar. It was the underbelly transportation method of choice to use on the series. Spinning and skidding the sleek machine on and off camera was what any good devil would do.

The first season went surprisingly smoothly. Scripts were finished and delivered in a timely fashion, and the cast soon became a family uniting in this strange, green experience. The attitude surrounding the project was as if we were all really breaking boundaries with the content, both on an emotional and a technological level. When filming outside of the studio, locations had included the exotic and strangely unfrequented industrial waste heaps of Los Angeles, as well as the tourist favorite, the twin towers of the downtown prison where we had taken our extremely attractive, barely dressed young female lead among the high-security inmates. Still, all went without a hitch, our lungs slightly more black and our underpants slightly more brown from the experiences.

We broke for the end of the season attending the lavish DEN Christmas party, hundreds of thousands of dollars in the making. Each patting one another on the back for our accomplishments of the year. Scantily clad women hung from the ceiling in cages, our show projected onto the wall of the dance floor as if a visual drug for the revelers as they danced the night away. Massive ice sculptures melted slowly around us as if they were tears flowing from the adoring public urging us to produce more shows.

And so we all anxiously waited for season two to commence.

DEN's management seemed happy, encouraging words still flowing from their well-trained lips. The cast seemed happy, money spilling from our pockets. Ratings seemed great, so now I took a more active role in generating dialogue and steering my character's trajectory. The writers welcomed input, happily releasing some of their creative control. As we began production on the second season, a sound that had previously been desperately muffled found its way into the audible whispers of the corridors. There were obviously some cutbacks in our budget, but nobody could really fathom why due to the collective positive gaggle shielding us all. I no longer had my own dressing room; I now shared with other members of the cast, as it was explained to me, to "keep up the team spirit." The words were spoken with uncertainty from behind a huge white smile. Lunchtime edibles seemed a little more sparse, as it was explained to me, to allegedly "keep us looking fit and healthy." And the show's main director and creator had been replaced, along with other key members of the team. This, on the other hand, was never explained to anyone.

Once filming properly resumed, scripts began being delivered page by page to add to the growing confusion. The verbose passages they intended me to vocalize became more and more ridiculous. Pages of dialogue were thrown into my hand minutes before I was about to recite passages I had memorized, changing absolutely everything. Still, we all battled on. I creatively placed my dialogue on inanimate objects around the set so I could at least read the dialogue thrust upon me. Unable to physically memorize anything that quickly, this became my only desperate solution. We all struggled through. I wrote passages on my hands; other actors tried by mouthing dialogue from behind the camera. All in all I was a complete and utter mess. I was flailing in front of a camera, due to no fault of my own, and I felt absolutely pathetic. Suddenly, I found myself so very alone amid the crowd.

Driving to in the mornings to the studio I had loved became a long and winding trudge. This wasn't in the slightest bit fun anymore. This was just hard work. I was now in a state of living fearfully yet at the same time bizarrely hoping that I would be released from the project, my services and multiple cockups no longer required. I had never dreamed I would feel this way after achieving what I had set forth from England to do. This was all so very wrong, in every possible way. And then my prayers were answered. Divine intervention—or probably more appropriately, devilish manipulation—placed an abrupt end to my suffering.

The fuck-up that was happening was actually coming from much higher up than anyone had anticipated. I arrived at the gates of the North Hollywood studio to find them padlocked, staff aimlessly milling around in the crisp early morning air. To everyone's surprise, the enterprising, bespeckeled creators were no more. Their buzzwords were no more. Their pasty-toned flesh had been replaced with the red flush of overwhelming embarrassment. DEN in its entirety was no more. And to the horror of many seated in board rooms, the investor millions were also no more.

Talk of the financial demise of DEN had been laughed off hours before by the founders, but really the only people they were conning were themselves. Days before the implosion of the network, one of the creatives had promptly resigned after a lawsuit was filed alleging he had been engaged in a sexual relationship with a *very* young boy. His dreams of being a Hollywood mogul had ended as quickly as they had started. We also learned that in addition to his appetite for minors, he also had a nasty habit of paying himself, and various pretty teen employees, seven-figure salaries, astronomical even for the decadent dot-com era. Their technological promise of so much was now so very little.

In Stanley Kubrick's film *2001*, technology and man stunningly collide, which resonated strongly with me over this whole experience. In the film, artificial intelligence suffers a severe malfunction. At DEN, basic human intelligence malfunctioned with severe consequences. By May 2000, the DEN project was completely broke. Terminated by the simple switch of a button. Just like in the movie.

Paying out huge salaries, for lavish parties, and for other misfired forms of hype and sexual deviance, DEN was bled quickly, like a hemophiliac, of its investors' large resources. The founders dissipated, regrouping somewhere, I'm sure, with the hope of generating a new batch of buzzwords and donning a new wardrobe to aid in their eternal disguises.

My blossoming career in this wave of the future was pulled out from under me along with any stability I had mistakenly presumed. The apparent sixty-five hundred hours' worth of programming created by DEN's various productions were left on a bankruptcy office floor in a nondescript Hollywood office building. The network's programming was sadly auctioned off years later in its entirety for a few thousand dollars. Obviously, the right buzzwords were not put forth in the auctions' advertising material.

Then again, DEN's buzzword-management masters were nowhere to be found.

CHAPTER TWENTY-THREE

≈

IT'S A WONDERFUL LIFE, 1946

Directed by Frank Capra.
George Bailey (James Stewart) spends his life giving up his dreams for
the good of his town, Bedford Falls. On Christmas Eve he is suicidal over
the misplacing of an $8,000 loan in his workplace. His guardian angel,
Clarence, falls to Earth and shows George how his town, family, and friends
would have turned out if he had never been born. George realizes that he
means a lot to very many people and sees that it really is a wonderful life.

The Hollywood Hills that encompass me are a perfect metaphor of the highs and lows for every actor on his or her journey. They are beautiful, lush, and inviting, seemingly easily scaled and palpable to the highest peak. Their hidden dangers and complexities have deceived many, myself now included. Be careful of what dreams you pray for in life. Sometimes you may get what you desire.

While still a youth, being thrown and molded slowly into the man of my life, I assumed that my dreams were to be handed to me. Stars would align and the heavens would play out destiny. I really had no choice in the matter. I lived with the undeniable security that I would continue on, innocent and full of dreams perpetually. In the journey I subsequently conjured up for myself, it seemed as though absolutely everything was plausible. My only limits were the far boundaries of my vivid imagination. This confident utopia housed me happily for years. Actually having to work at my dream, though, I soon discovered that doubt sought to diminish my assurance in absolutely everything.

Upon this moment of reflection, the night's moon is silver and full, as if a hand from the heavens were delicately taking time to light Hollywood in its entirety. The sound of supposed security, the humming of a police helicopter somewhere looking down upon me is a constant in this strange land, protecting the city's hopes and dreams. The humming blends seamlessly into melodies drifting along, penetrating my thoughts through my broken bedroom window. The songs travel in on bumpy waves across the heavy, humid air, each song with its own memory, a musical timeline for the journey taken thus far; a strange compilation of experiences. A jumbled, never-ending soundtrack to my life.

I came to Hollywood seeking a deeper meaning, a challenge for my creativity, and, most importantly, a true home. A city that would encourage and support the dream I had carried as far back as I could remember from the dirty gray streets of London. I was finally at home, I assured myself, living among my documented successes and failures, in my current curious surroundings. Light loses its battle once more to dark as the night progresses ruthlessly onward. I can hear my neighbor's television through the thinness of the wall as he enthusiastically shouts along with a Steven Seagal movie. I would like to think that irony, and not actually anything that Steven Seagal is doing intentionally, brings a smile to my face. My smile and the thought of Seagal are undeniably coexisting, signaling, surely, that the end of days is nigh.

It seems that when I reached the sandy white shores of this land everything was very familiar to me. A form of endless déjà vu, as if this is where my life's path had been directing me constantly. I had landed in a country in which I felt I could still fulfill my potential on life's fight with acceptance, and the pursuit of societal success. It was a fight I battled often. I ultimately discovered that I was struggling in a conflict that was only with myself. I had already achieved success; I had nothing to prove to anyone else. Success for me had simply been the courage to actually live my dream. A dream I awoke from nightly, and happily now pursued daily. I had been finally *admitted* into the beginnings of my true life's calling. I was barely at the foot of the Hollywood Hills, staring up at the highest peak, and it felt wonderful.

The general perception of a successful actor is, unfortunately, a misguided one in Hollywood. The combination of money, fame, and high-profile projects that are associated with a successful career, in fact, defines an entirely different profession—that of a celebrity. My alter ego had played this fantasy role from as far back as I could remember. I was VERY famous in my mind from the instant of my first glimpse of a film; I was just waiting patiently for the rest of the world to catch on to my insight. In my reality, though, I wasn't a movie star or any kind of icon, far from it, but this had never been my true aspiration. What I was, was an actor, and at last I was proud to call it my profession.

Living here in this city of film you discover many facades. Movies are a pure illusion, the illusion beginning with the very word itself—movie. There really is in literal terms no such thing as a motion picture. A moving, talking piece of celluloid just doesn't exist. What we really stare at are still photographs—twenty-four brief flickers of images per second, inevitably summoning a multitude of thoughts, feelings, and actions from within ourselves. A place in which each of us has a unique documentary taking shape, where one's own personal life story begins to play out for the world.

The films I watched growing up might not have all been great films but they all filled me with grandiose thoughts. From

187

its humble, animated *Jungle Book* beginnings, my mind had been opened to endless possibilities. People in general want to be moved when they buy a ticket to a film. They enter the cinema with an open heart and mind hoping to be in some way emotionally affected, an openness that is unfortunately rare in today's cynical society. It was the one place as I was growing up in which it was perfectly acceptable to laugh, scream, cry, or cheer—in fact, it was encouraged. There was never any judgment passed by society while within those hallowed walls.

Film's true relevance is not just "a simple form of entertainment," a fact many will spew at the slightest of opportunities (a point not helped by Randy Quaid's illustrious career). Film is and has always been more than just a frivolous way to spend a couple of hours of your spare time. The Supreme Court of the United States of America has stated that film is a "significant medium for the communication of ideas." It has proved itself as one of the most effective forms of mass communication ever devised. Film's impact on society and communication should therefore never be underestimated. It is so much more than just an opportunity to cry at some Disney sing-along extravaganza.

The 1942 film *Mrs. Miniver* was deemed so powerful by the American President Franklin Delano Roosevelt that he ordered dialogue from the film to be printed on leaflets and dropped over occupied Nazi Germany by Allied forces. Film holds the power to alter a person's thinking, juxtaposing the huge world and one's small place in it, as it did to me in London as a child every single week, wide-eyed and ready to learn. Most intriguingly, though, it holds within its transfixing, flickering light the possibility of pure imagination. Nothing could be more important. Nothing was more important to me.

Who knows what scenarios are still to unspool across the flickering lamplights of each of our imaginations? The future that each and every one of us faces, touched and altered in some way after every cinematic experience.

Movies really do make a difference in society.

Movies really do mean something.

Movies have always meant *everything* to me.

I know these facts now more than ever in my heart of hearts, working and living a life in film.

I have heard my friends left behind in England mutter at various times in their lives that they had awakened from an alcoholic haze to find middle-age coldly staring back, losing any semblance of ambition. They find themselves living day to day with the nagging notion of "What if...?" What if the purpose of their mediocre-at-best lives is only to serve as a warning to others? That now their destiny holds nothing more than bitterness and missed opportunity. I, on the other hand, have never felt the loss of my life. I was always on a very clear straight path in a landscape that was very familiar, lit brightly by the golden rays of the California sun. I had already visited my final destination every weekend on the cinematic screen. I knew this land before me as though it was an old, familiar, comforting friend. This truly was becoming a wonderful life.

The little golden tickets I was presented with each and every weekend at the cinema doors in Croydon by the decrepit ticket collector Stubby had been a clear indicator of my destiny. If only I had taken the time to really understand the message he placed with love carefully into the palm of my tiny, unknowing hands.

ADMIT ONE the tickets would read.

ADMIT ONE into this cinematic fantasy world.

It just took me a long time to piece the torn paper stubs back together, so I could clearly understand my true dream. I had at last begun to find in myself happiness, a true home living among my one true childhood pleasure that still surrounded me daily. People still congregate in Hollywood more than anywhere else on Earth with a passion and a unique vision. A town of true dreamers and ambitious transients. Leaving all they know behind, trying to make themselves a home where creatively they can be happy and thrive as I myself did.

My true journey had in fact only just begun. My experiences so far had ultimately been nothing more than preparation for the main attraction. Now all I needed to uncover was the longevity to hold onto my aspirations.

They say that middle age is a time where the clothes of life begin to fit people better. Luckily, I still had a full wardrobe full of costumes I was waiting to grow into with excited anticipation.

Only time will tell.

EPILOGUE

❧

My parents are still married, living in the same section of England that the family moved to when they took me away from London. They still take trips to the cinema, though now *they* sleep more often than they actually watch the films. They live proudly thinking they have raised the new *Brady Bunch*.

My hereditary dislike of my brother, Cymon, never changed. We rarely speak; in fact, we only speak when forced to. He lives in Cambridgeshire, unmarried to this day.

Both my adopted sisters grew up with their own troubles. Georgina became disturbed than anyone could have possibly imagined. She would leave my parents' home, having pulled a knife on my mother, and live for a short time a few streets away. She was soon arrested for drug possession and distribution. At nineteen years old she is currently serving her sentence in a women's prison.

My mother's father successfully smoked himself to death. My grandmother thought I would be back in England after a few weeks upon leaving for America, although she hoped for the best. She carried with her one wish, to watch me on the telly with the neighbors if I was really an actor. She died while I was filming what would become the biggest film of all time, having never seen me act.

My father's parents, now well in their eighties, continue to live a very disciplined life. They both do their best to fill their empty days, still rising at precisely 0600 hours.

Thomas Burns and Joanne Hardy were never to be heard of again. I like to think that Thomas somehow engineered his disappearance, waiting intentionally for the perfect moment to reappear with the trivia question to end all questions. Hopefully Joanne in her adult years is breast-feeding happily; it would be a travesty if this were not the case.

Graham Tonkin currently works at Gatwick airport, assisting people on their holiday getaways, having never left the area in which we were both happy children.

Stubby passed away quietly. He worked at the cinema in London up until the week he died, tearing tickets for countless thousands of lucky children with precision and great care.

Steven Seagal, surprisingly, continues to make movies.

Name EMMETT HUMPHRIES   Form 1.2   Subject DRAMA .

Ability Group MIXED   Term Grade C—   Exam /

Homework /   Progress GOOD   Behaviour SATISFACTORY

Comment: EMMETT DOES NEED TO THINK ABOUT VARYING THE TONE OF HIS VOICE WHEN HE SPEAKS.

Subject Teacher W. Tempan.

ABOUT THE AUTHOR

Emmett James spent his childhood in Croydon, South London,

and finished his schooling in Cambridge, England. Studying acting at Strasberg Actors Studio in London he began working in theater, eventually moving to Los Angeles in the early nineties to pursue his acting career in film and television. He has worked extensively as a thespian in every single medium, from voicing a #1 video game franchise to a recurring role on America's oldest-running soap opera. Projects he has lent his talents to have been honored with Golden Globe, SAG, Oscars, Emmy, and BAFTA awards. He was also presented with a prestigious ADA award for his work on the Los Angeles stage. In addition to acting, he has produced, taught, and directed film, stage, and television productions in Hollywood and London. Coming from a family of authors that includes J.B. Priestley, Emmett continues to live and work in Hollywood to this day.

TOP: From left, Cymon, complete with his *Jungle Book* grin, and me on my first day of school.
BOTTOM: From far right myself and Graham Tonkin on our beloved BMX bikes.

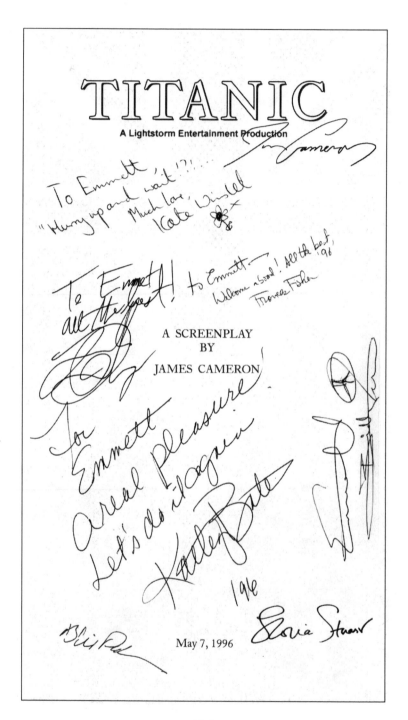

TITANIC

A Lightstorm Entertainment Production

To Emmett,
"Hurry up and wait !?!...
Much love,
Kate Winslet

To Emmett!
all the best!

to Emmett —
Welcome aboard! All the best,
'96
Frances Fisher

A SCREENPLAY
BY

JAMES CAMERON

For
Emmett
a real pleasure
Let's do it again
Kathy Bates
'96

May 7, 1996

Gloria Stuart

196